COLORING CREEPY HORROR MOVIES

AN UNOFFICIAL COLORING ADVENTURE

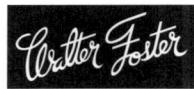

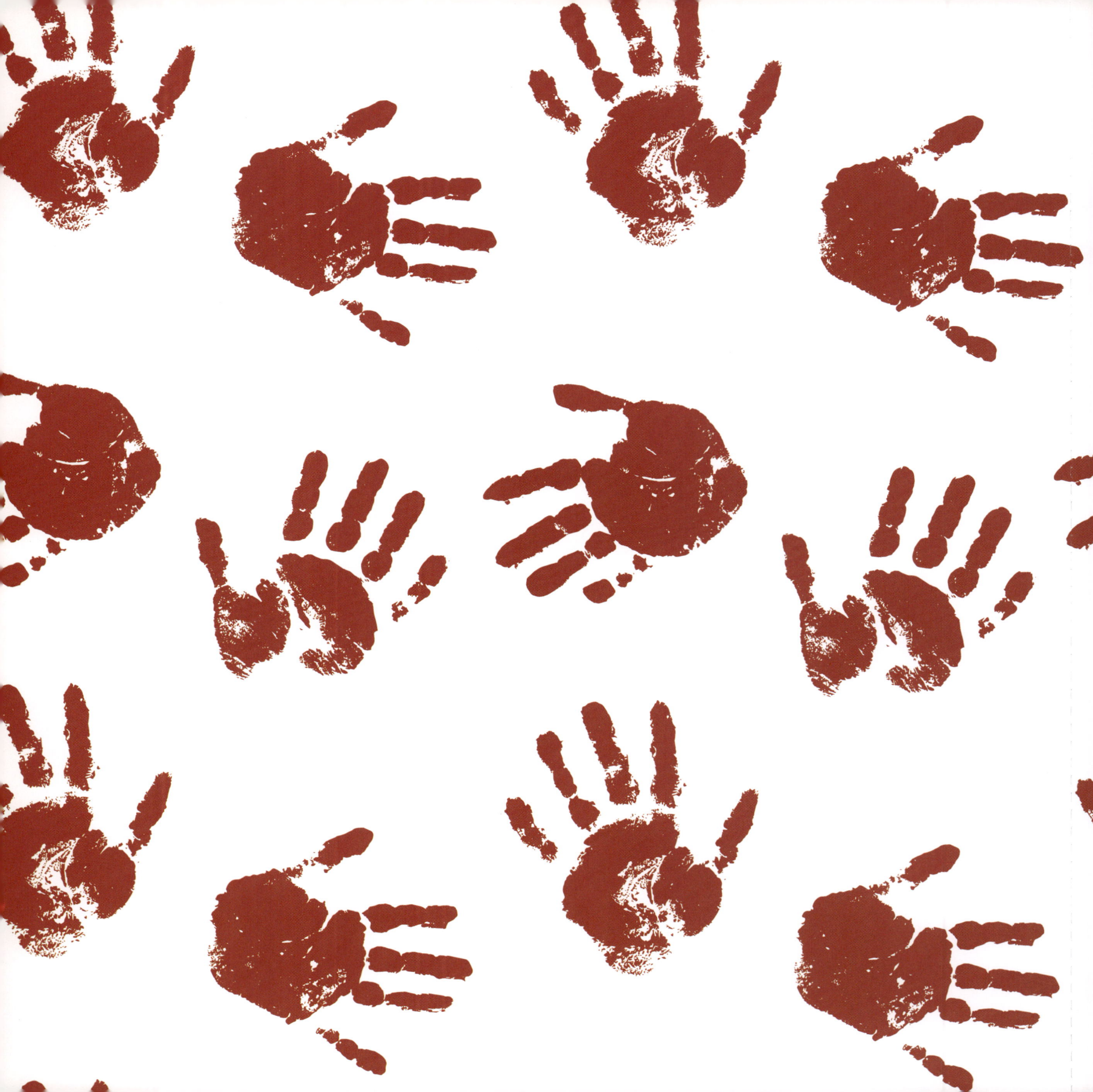

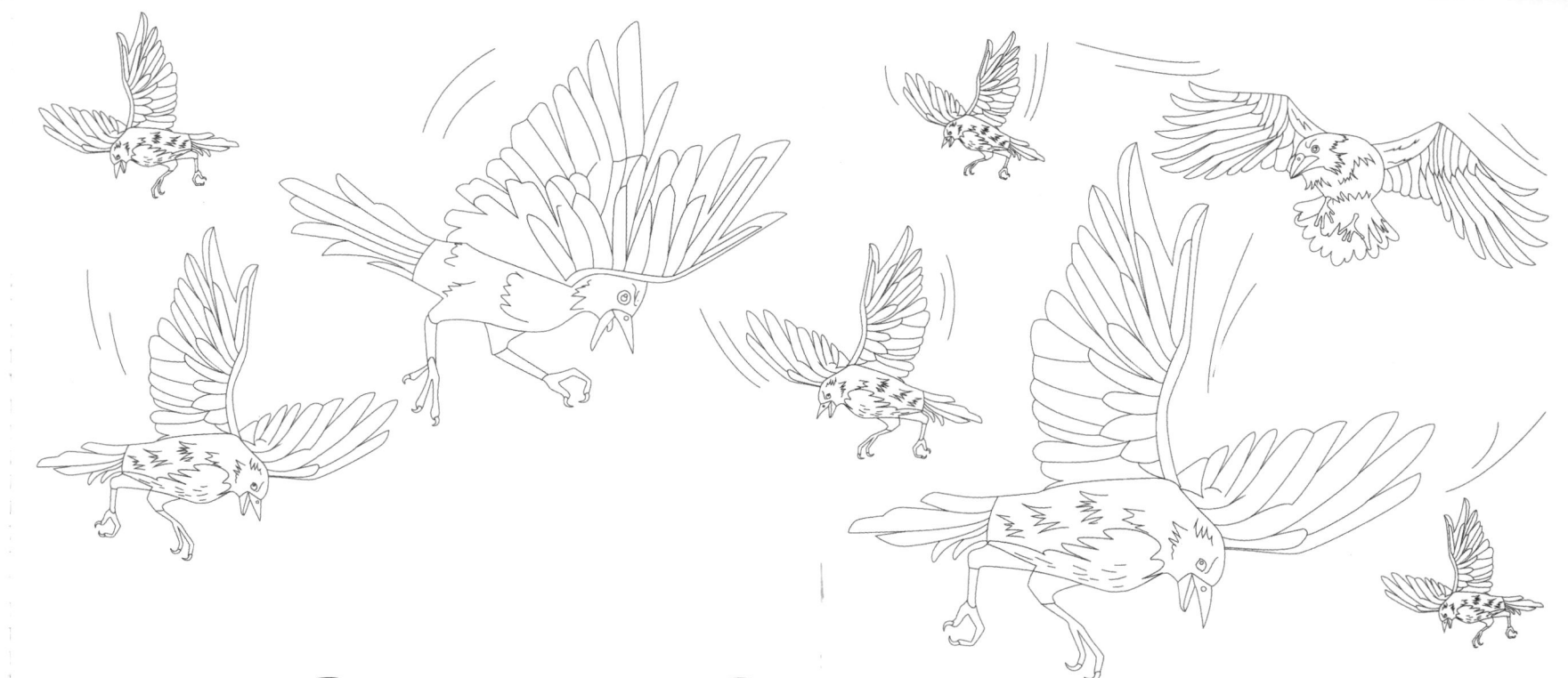

Dive into the Darkness with Your Favorite Frights

Coloring Creepy Horror Movies invites you to immerse yourself in eerie illustrations inspired by some of the most iconic horror films of all time. From sinister settings to unforgettable villains, this collection celebrates your favorite movie moments.

Printed on high-quality, perforated paper, these single-sided pages are perfect for displaying your finished masterpieces—if you dare. Whether you're a seasoned artist or just starting out, there's something for everyone to enjoy.

Tips for coloring:

- ✻ Experiment with your favorite coloring tools to get the effects you want.
- ✻ Relive the terror by coloring while you rewatch these classics.

Get ready to unleash your creativity while revisiting the scenes that made you scream!

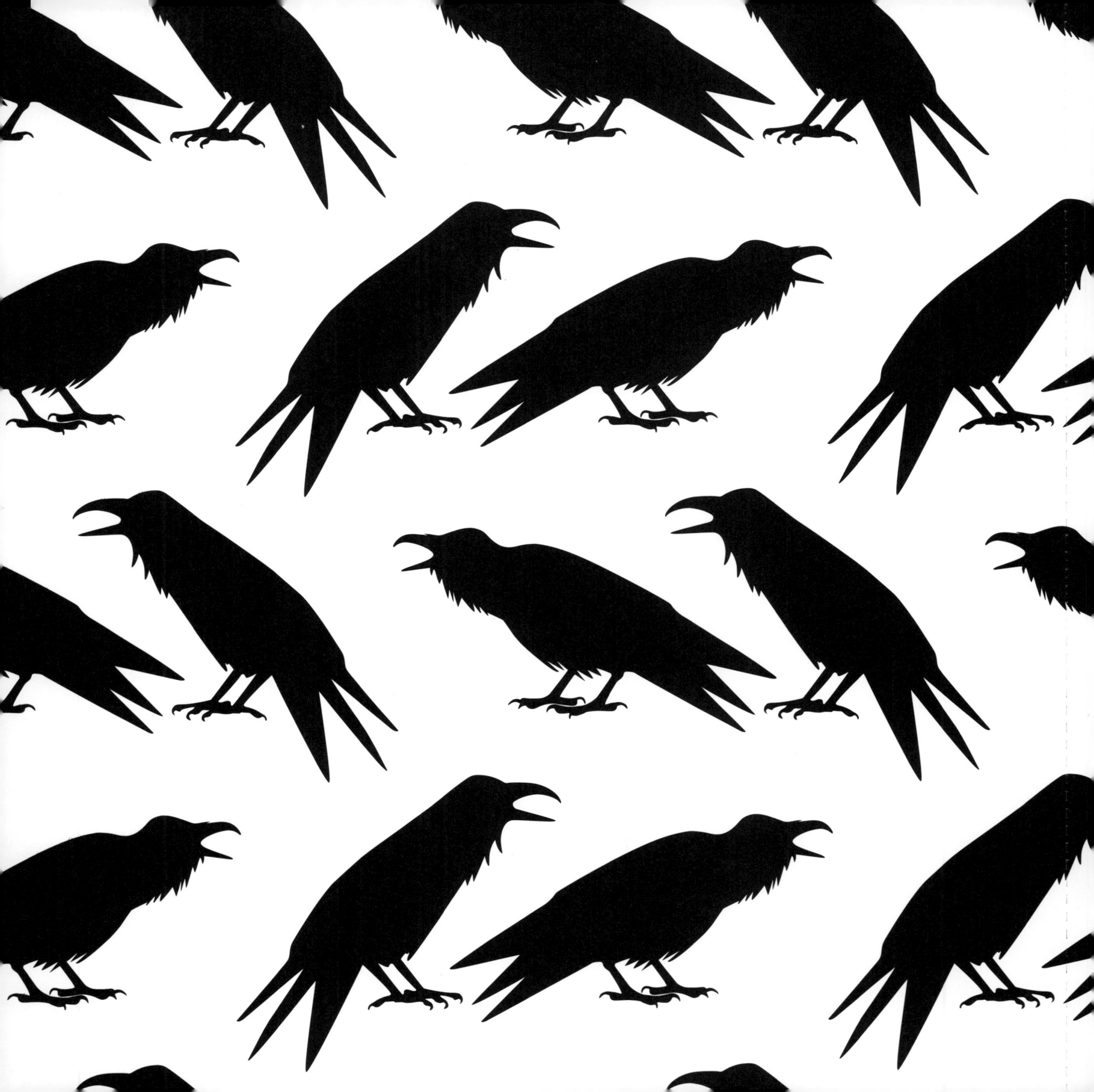

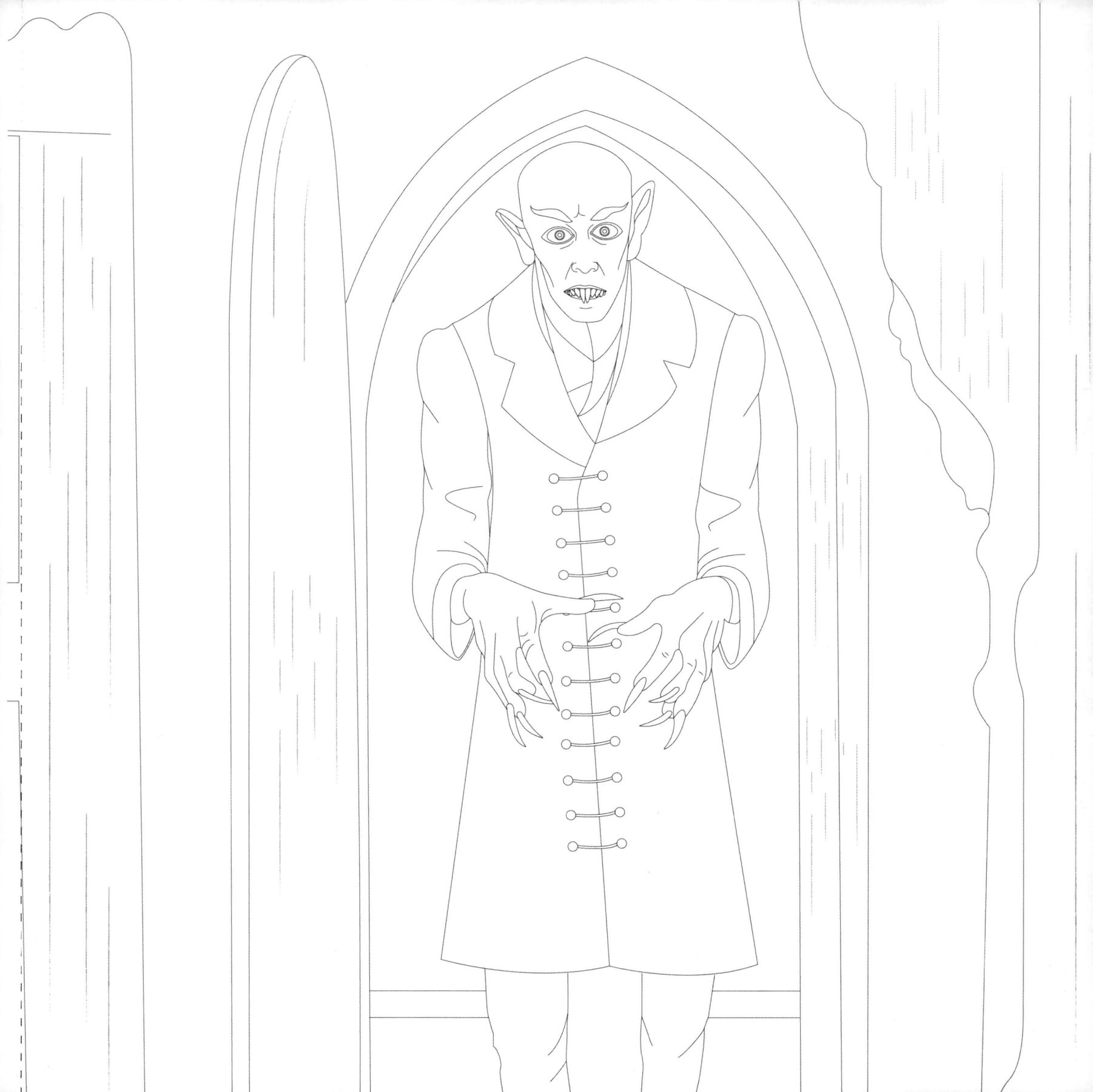

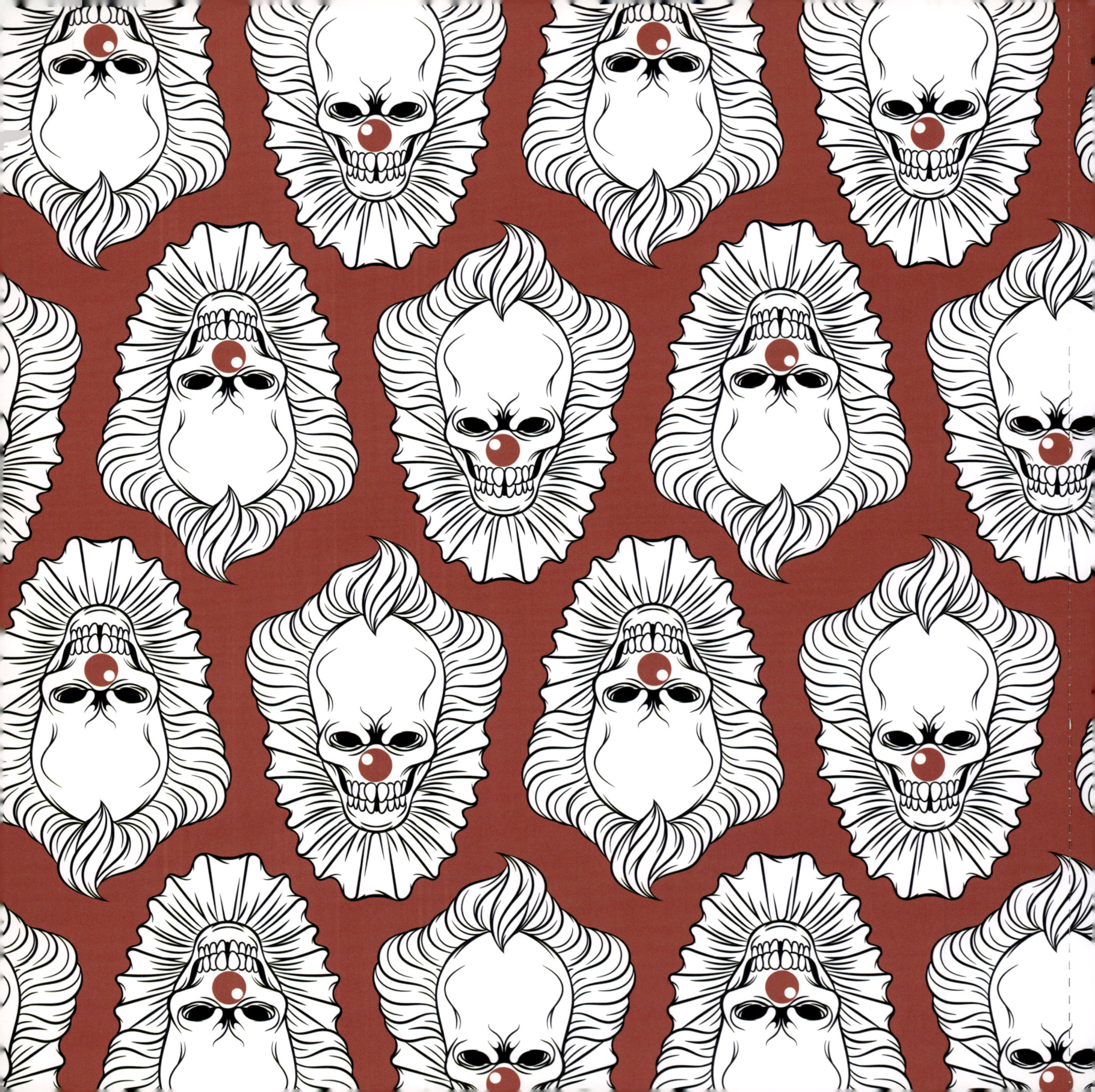

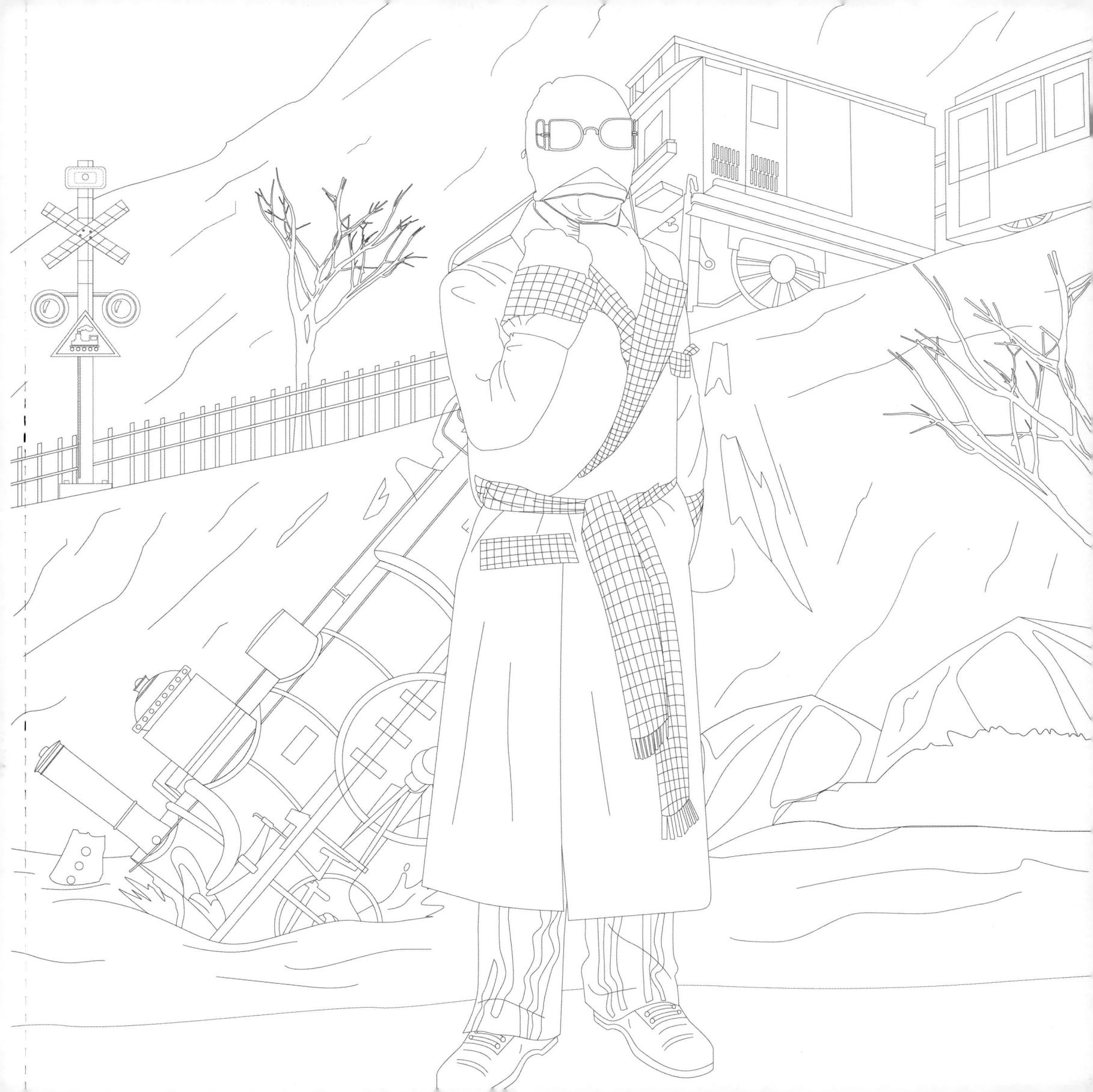

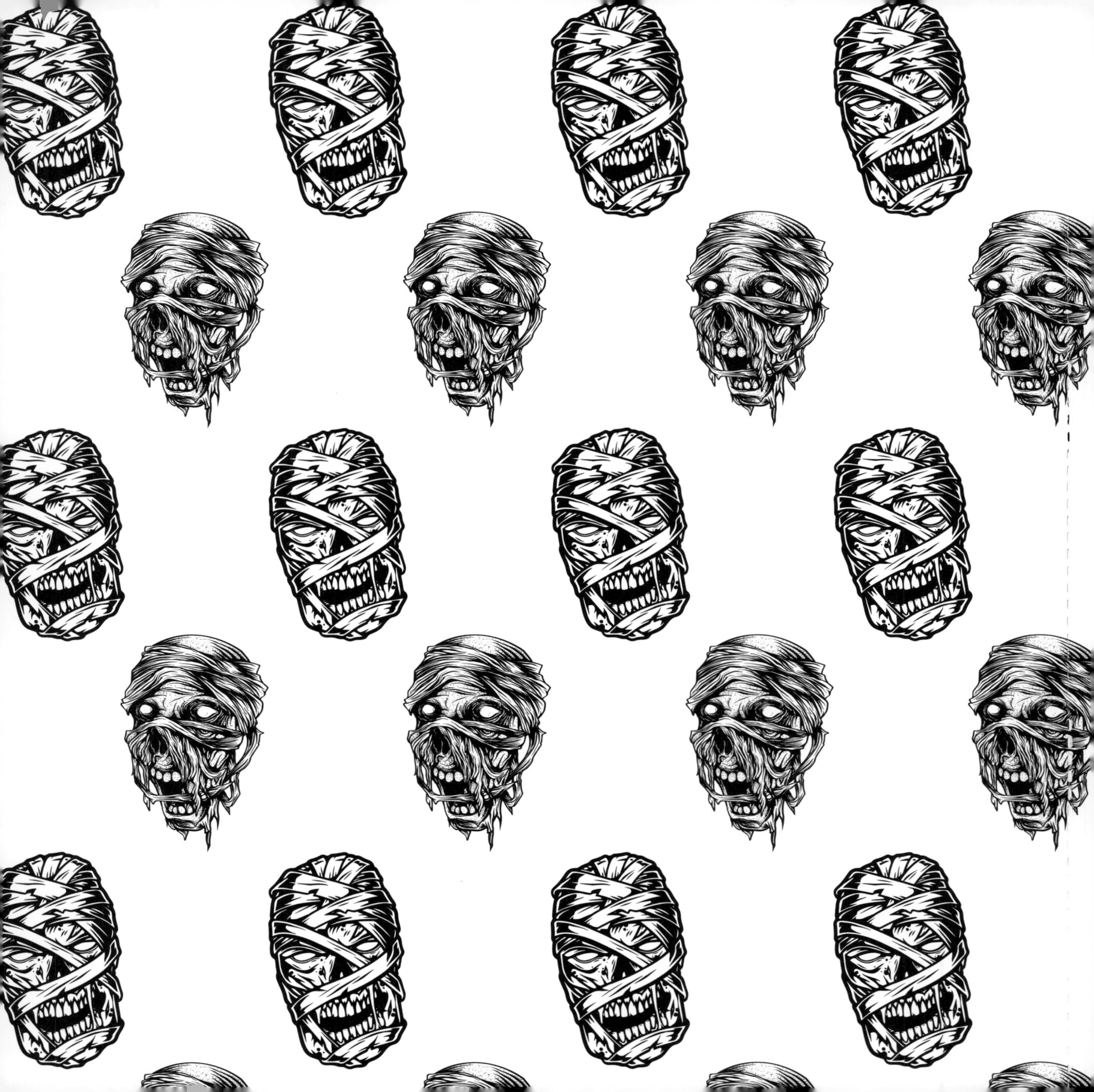

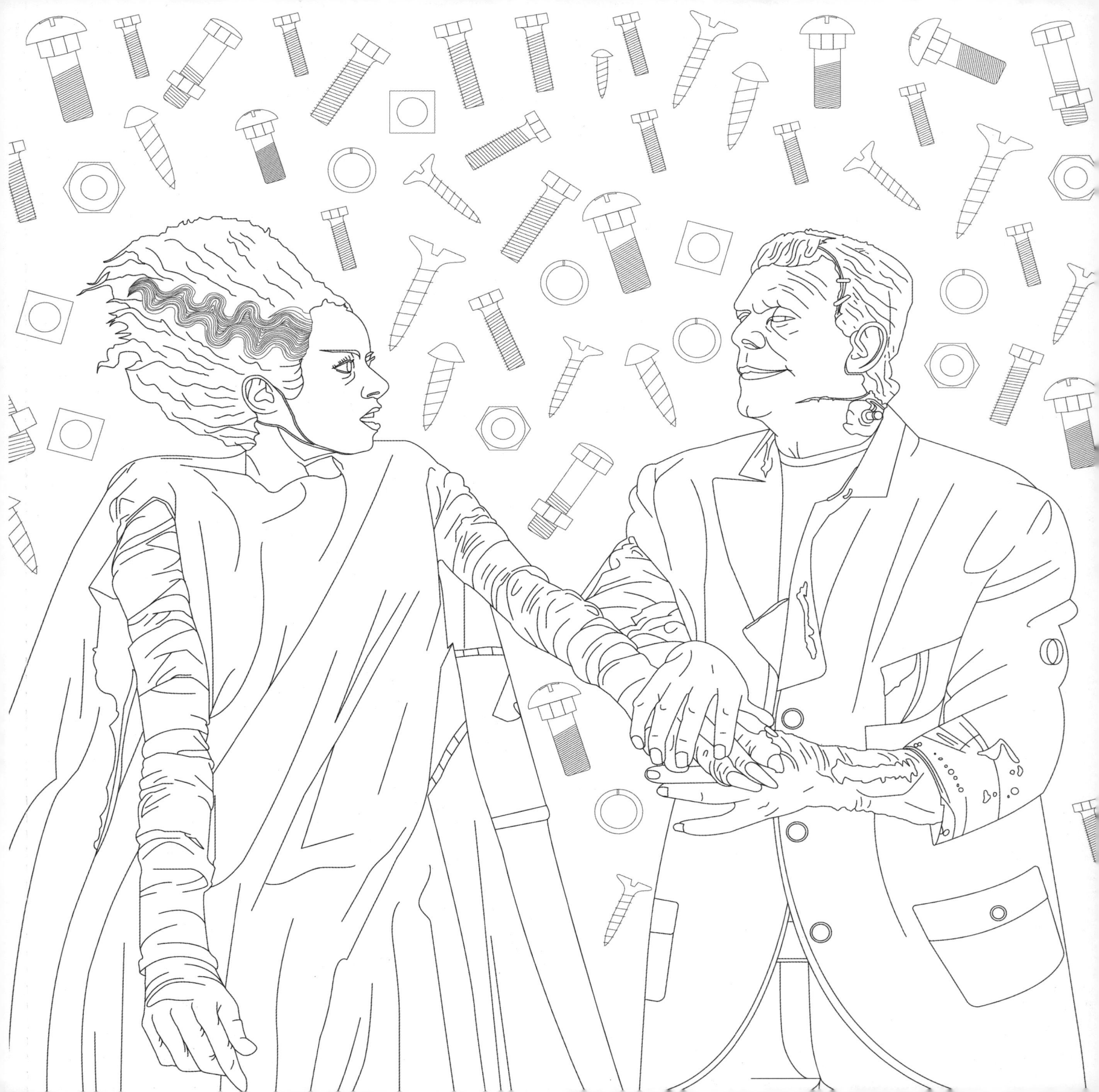

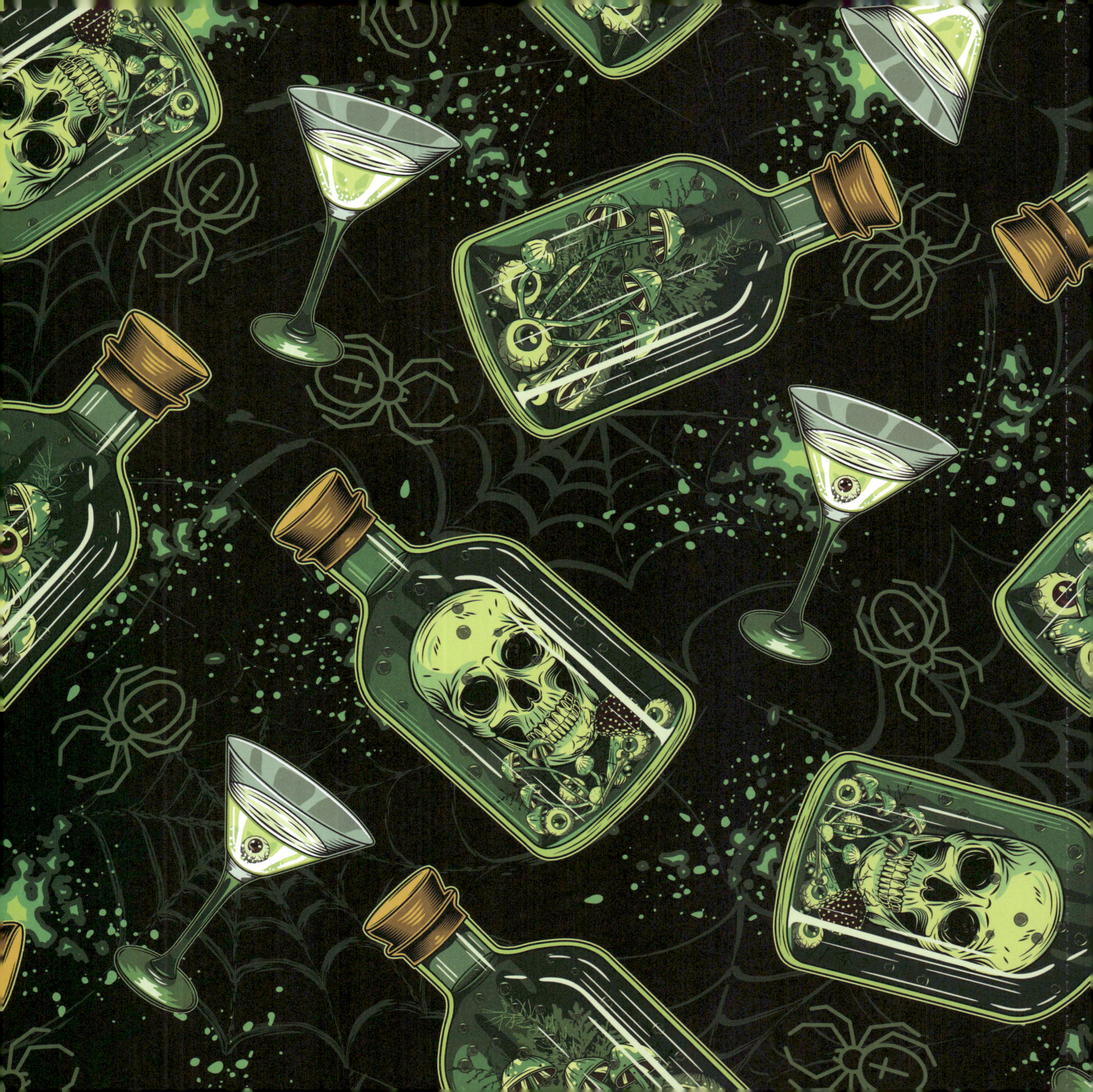

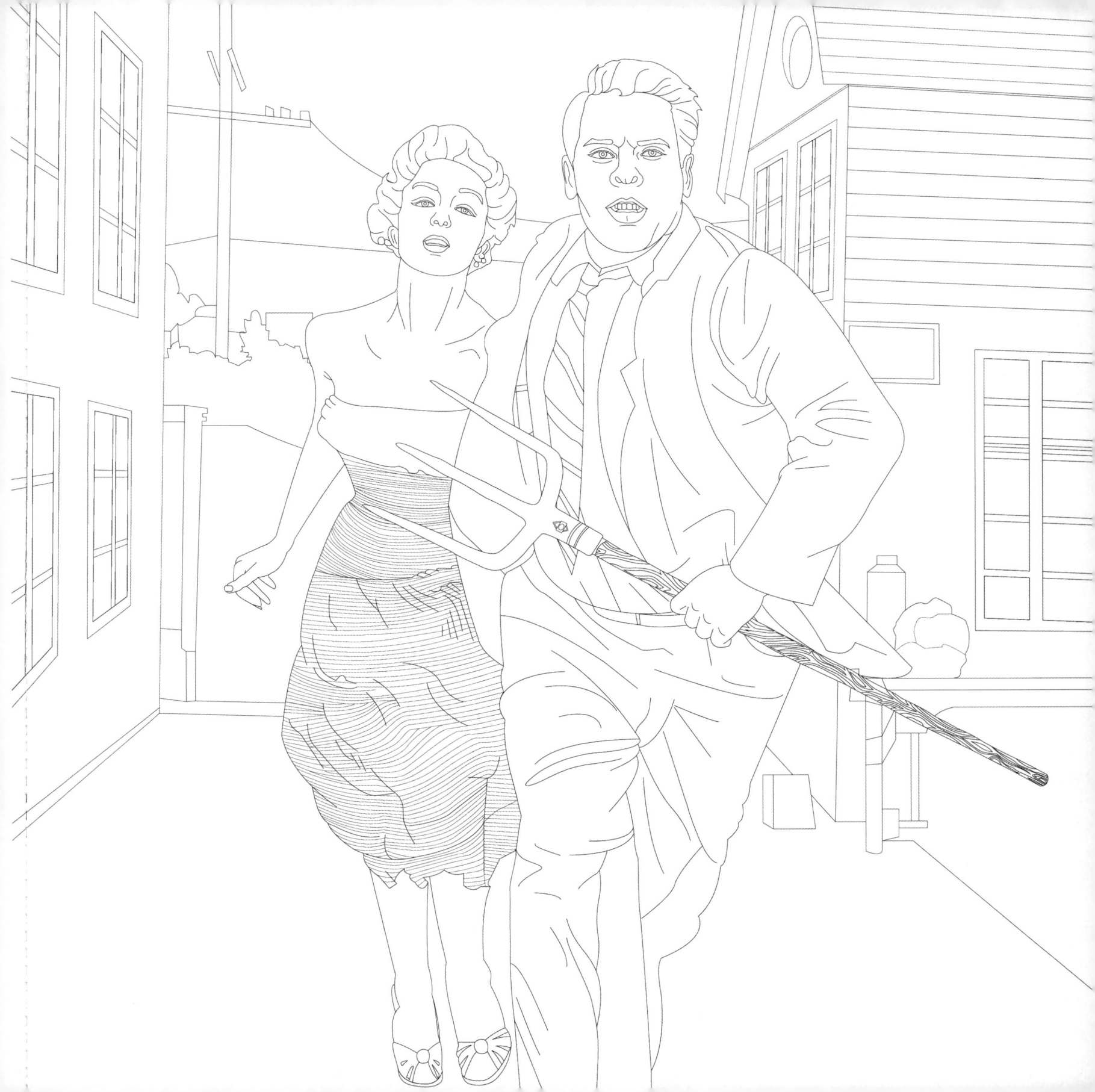

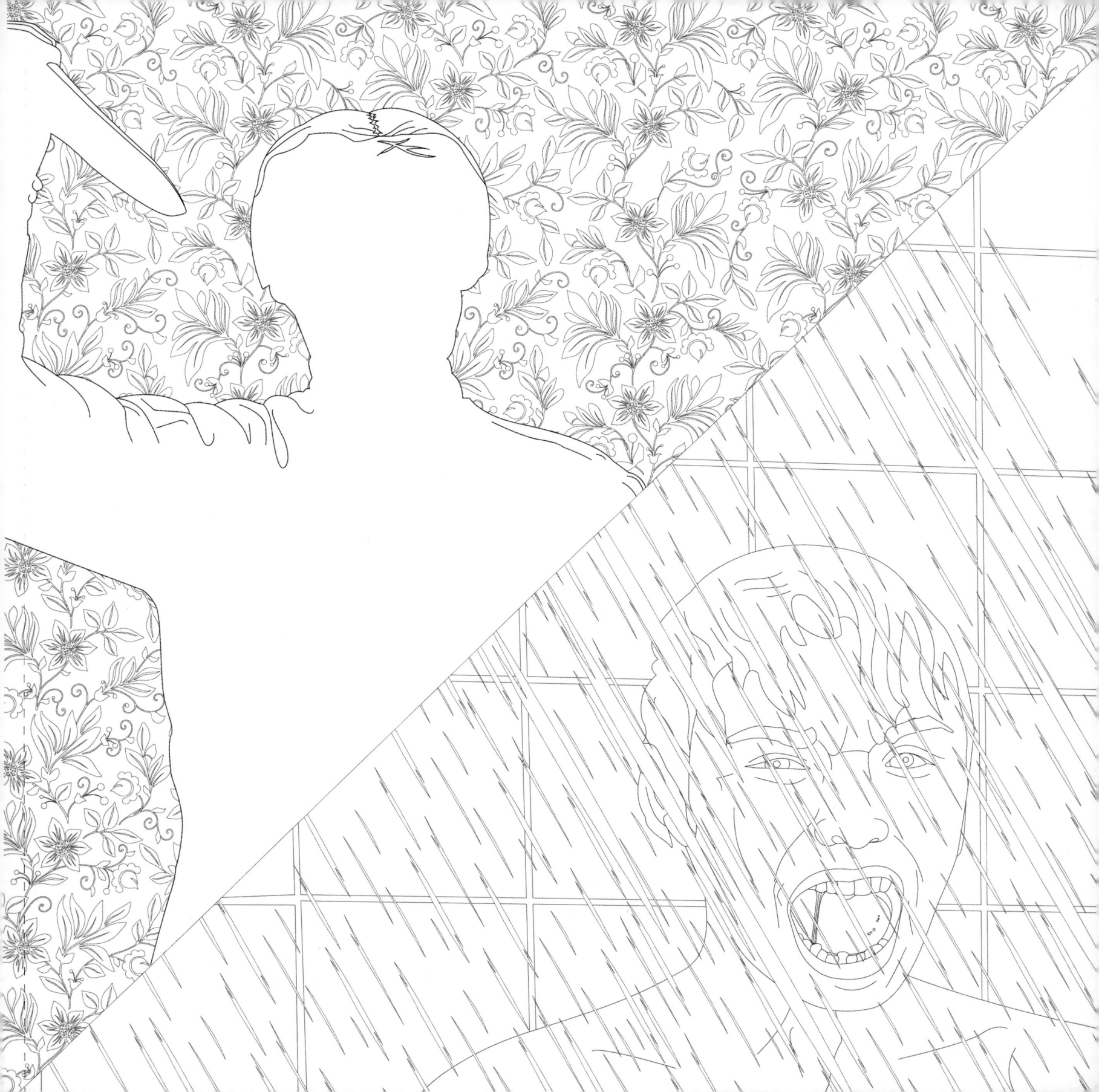

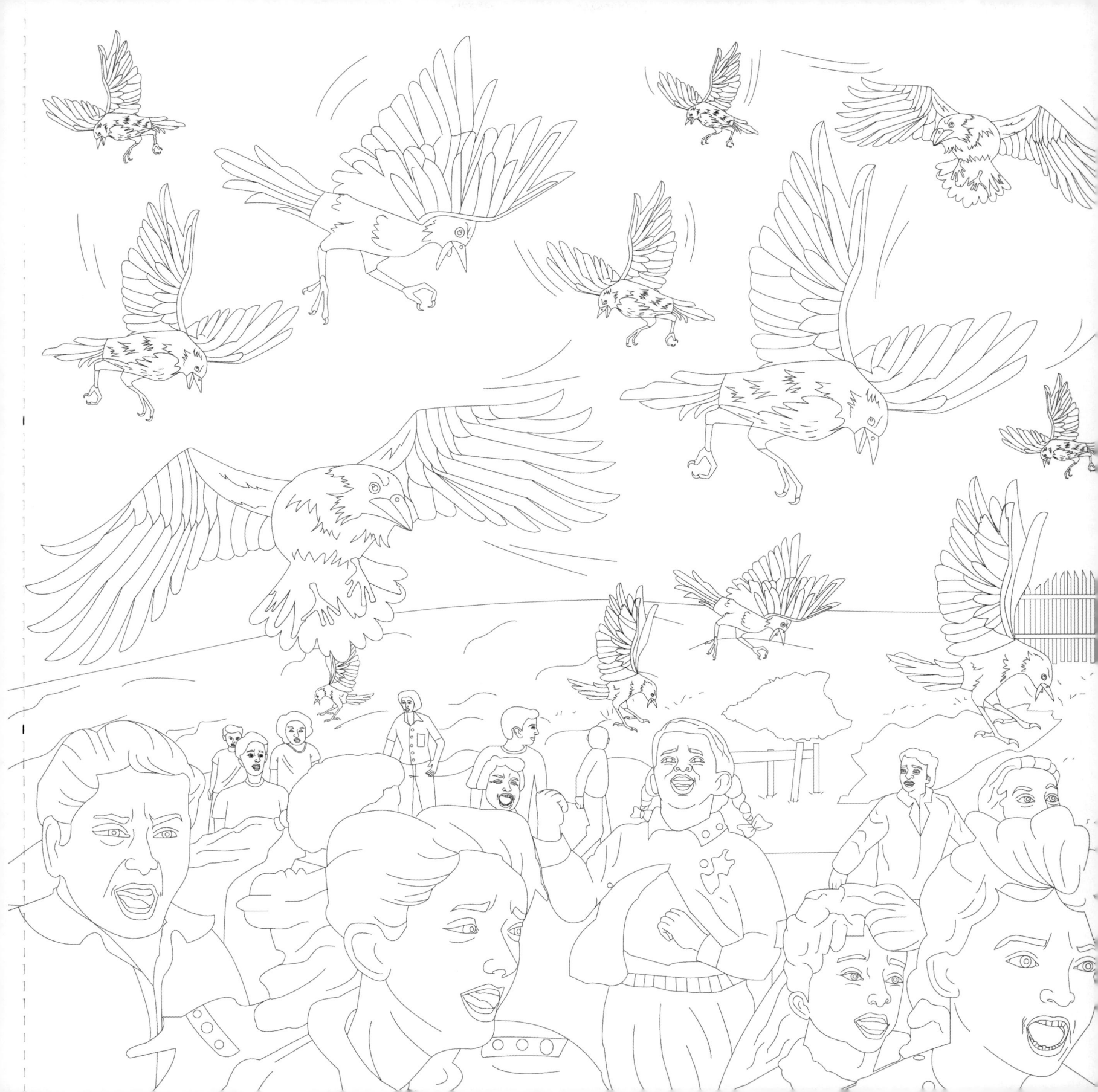

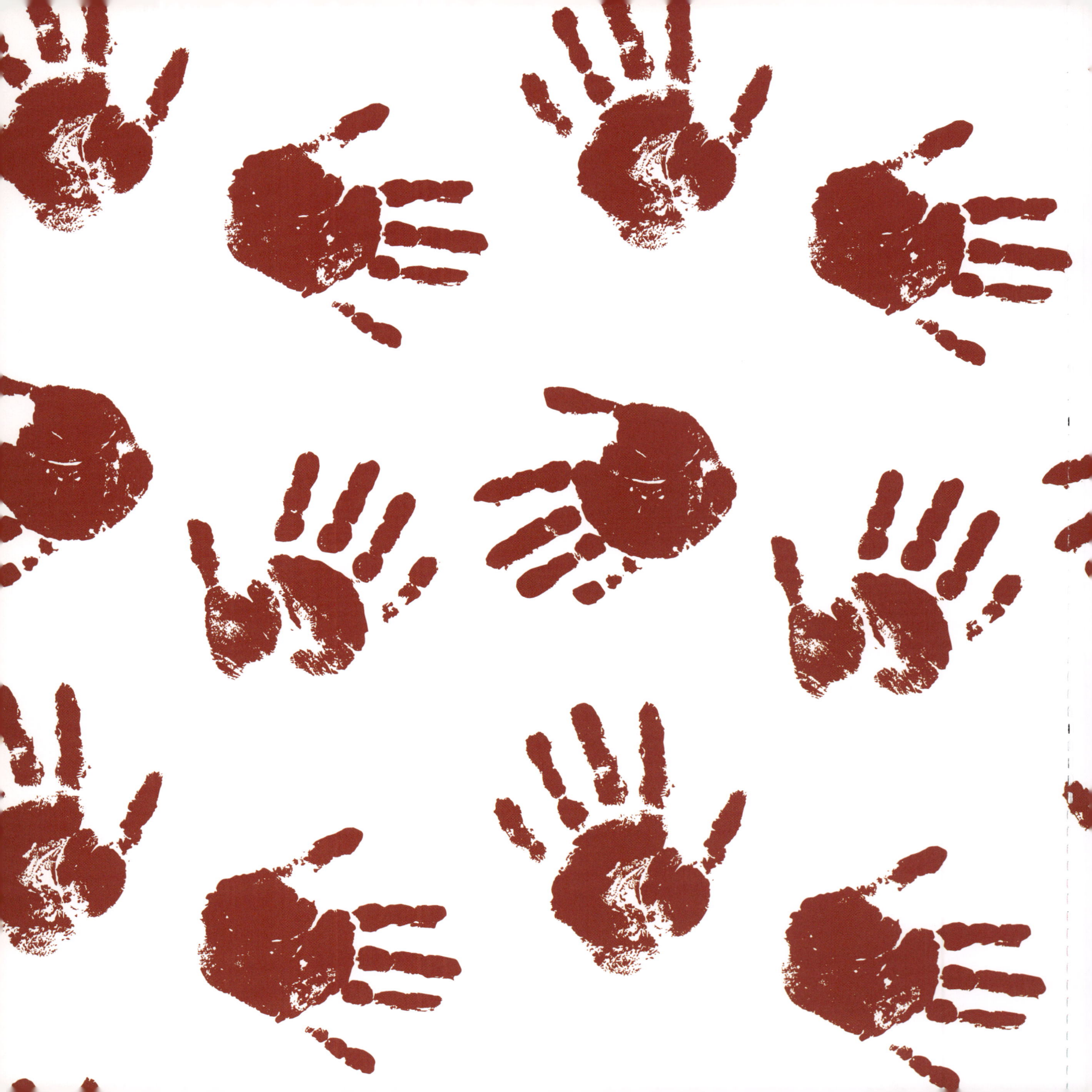

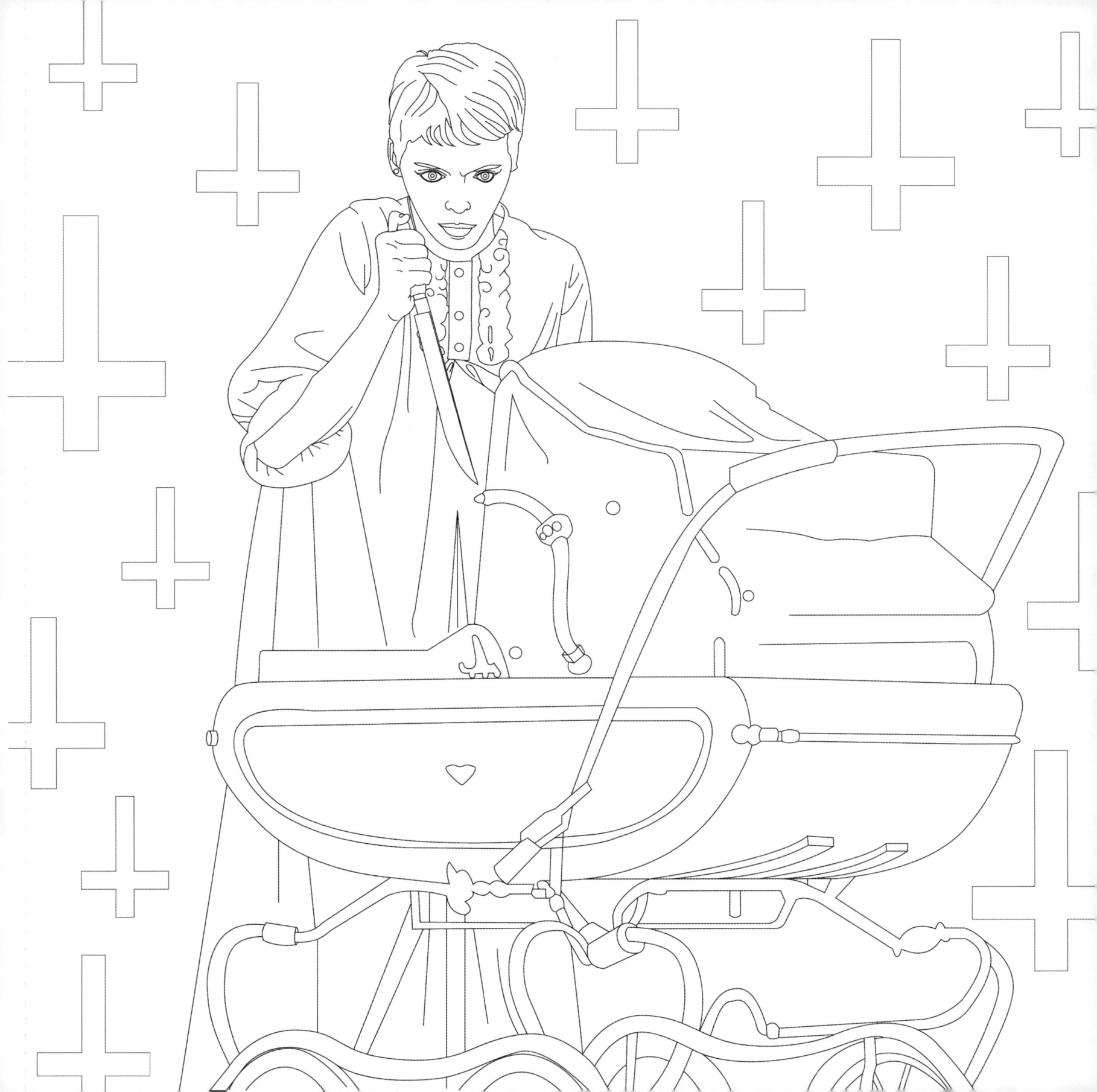

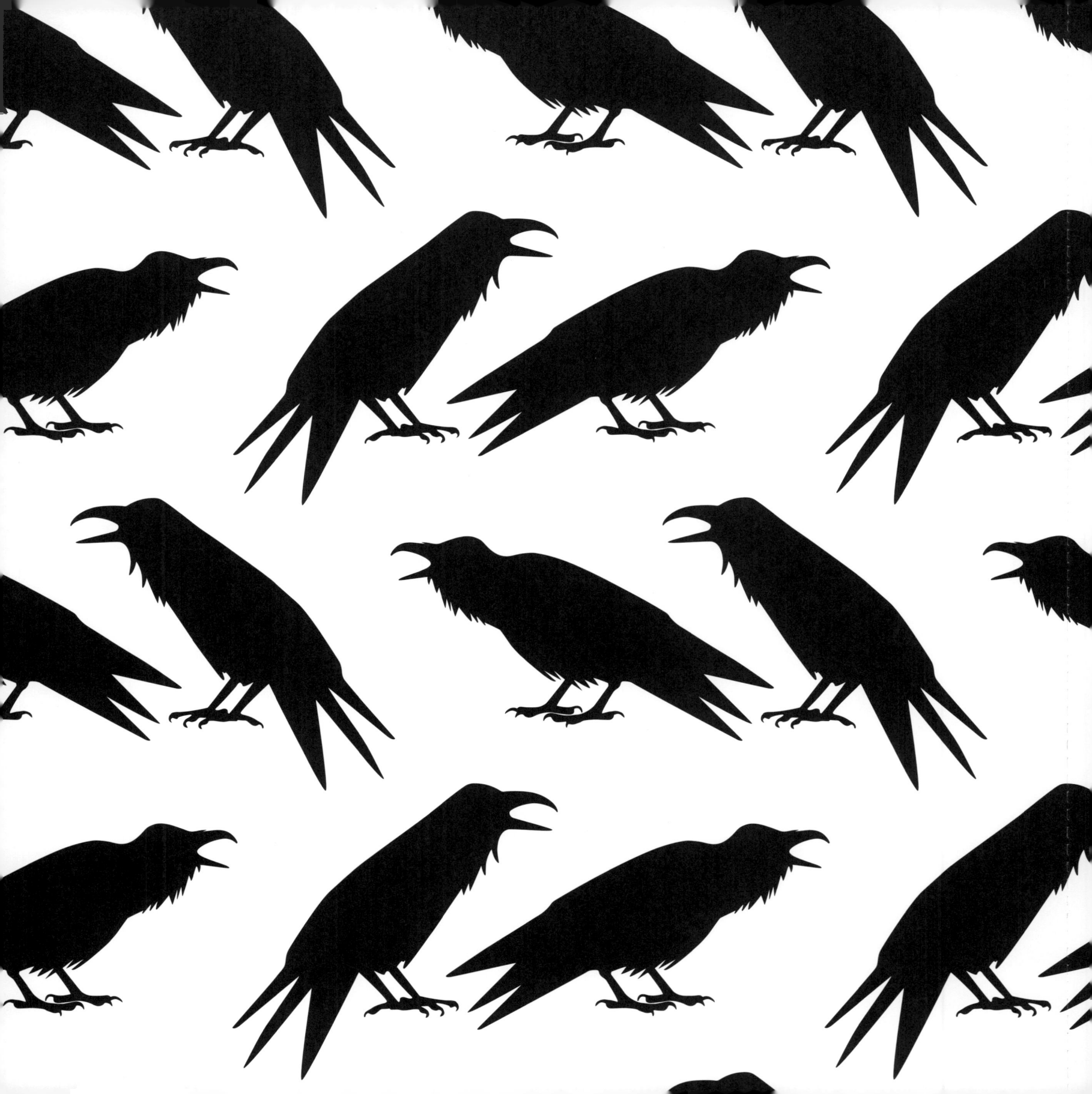

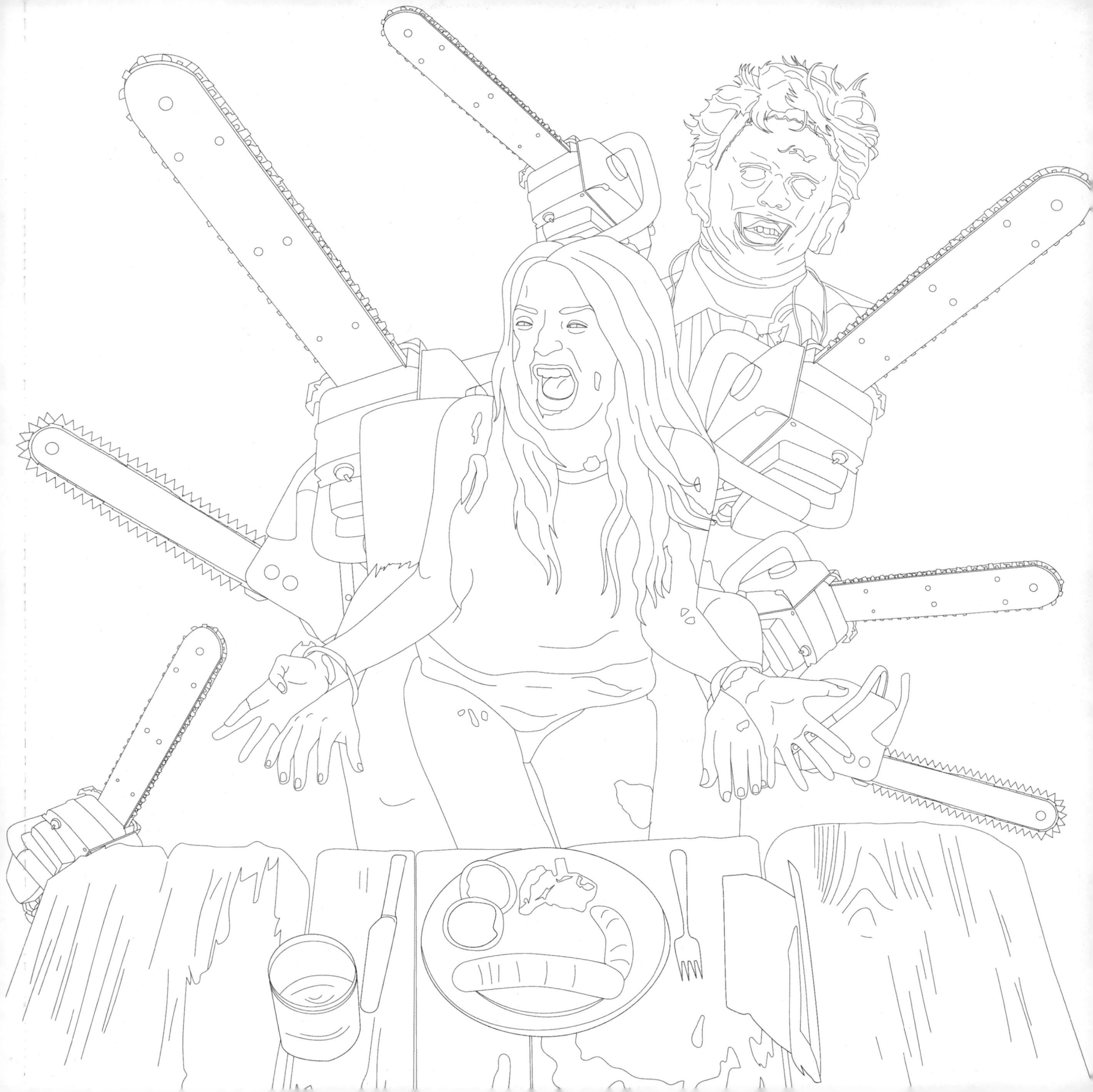

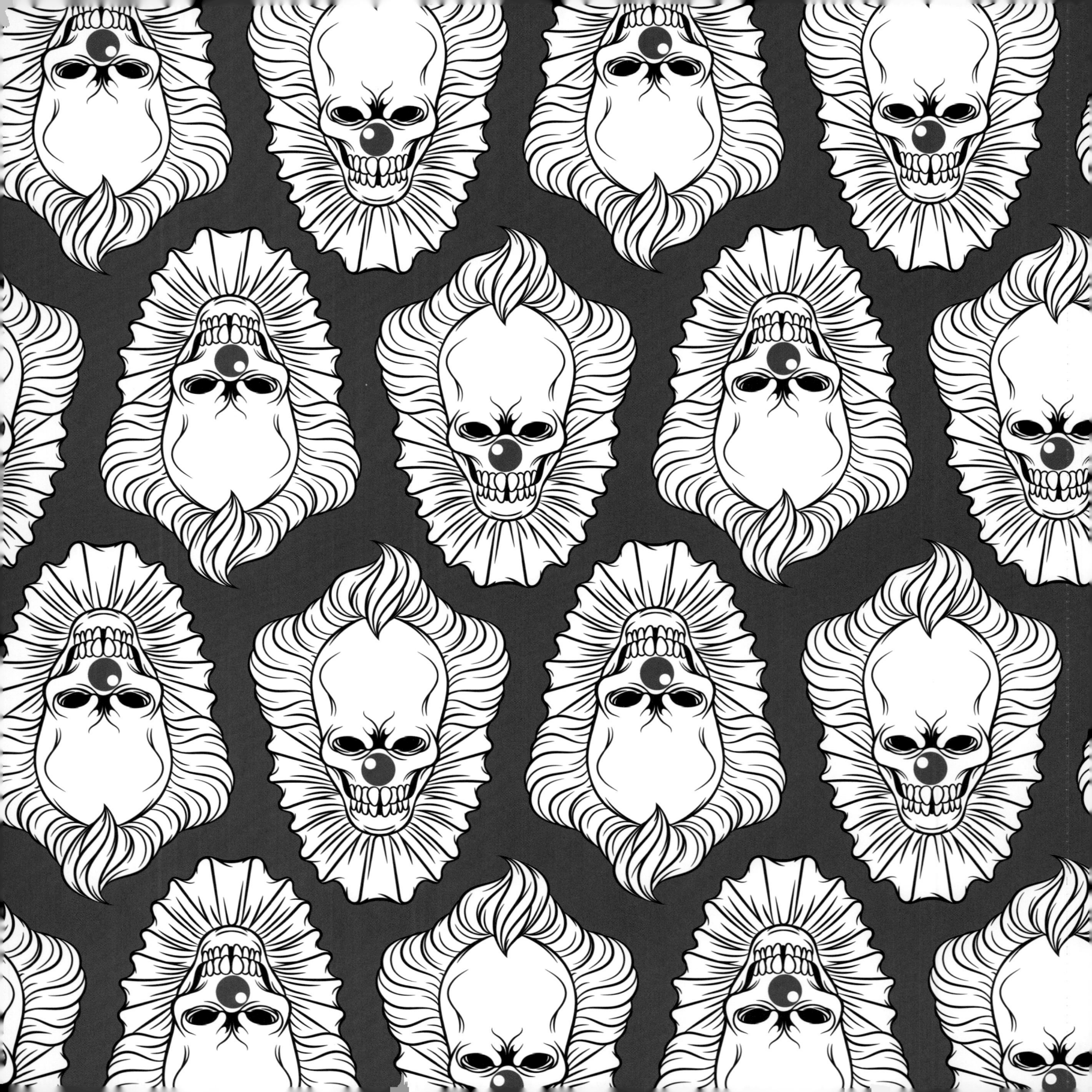

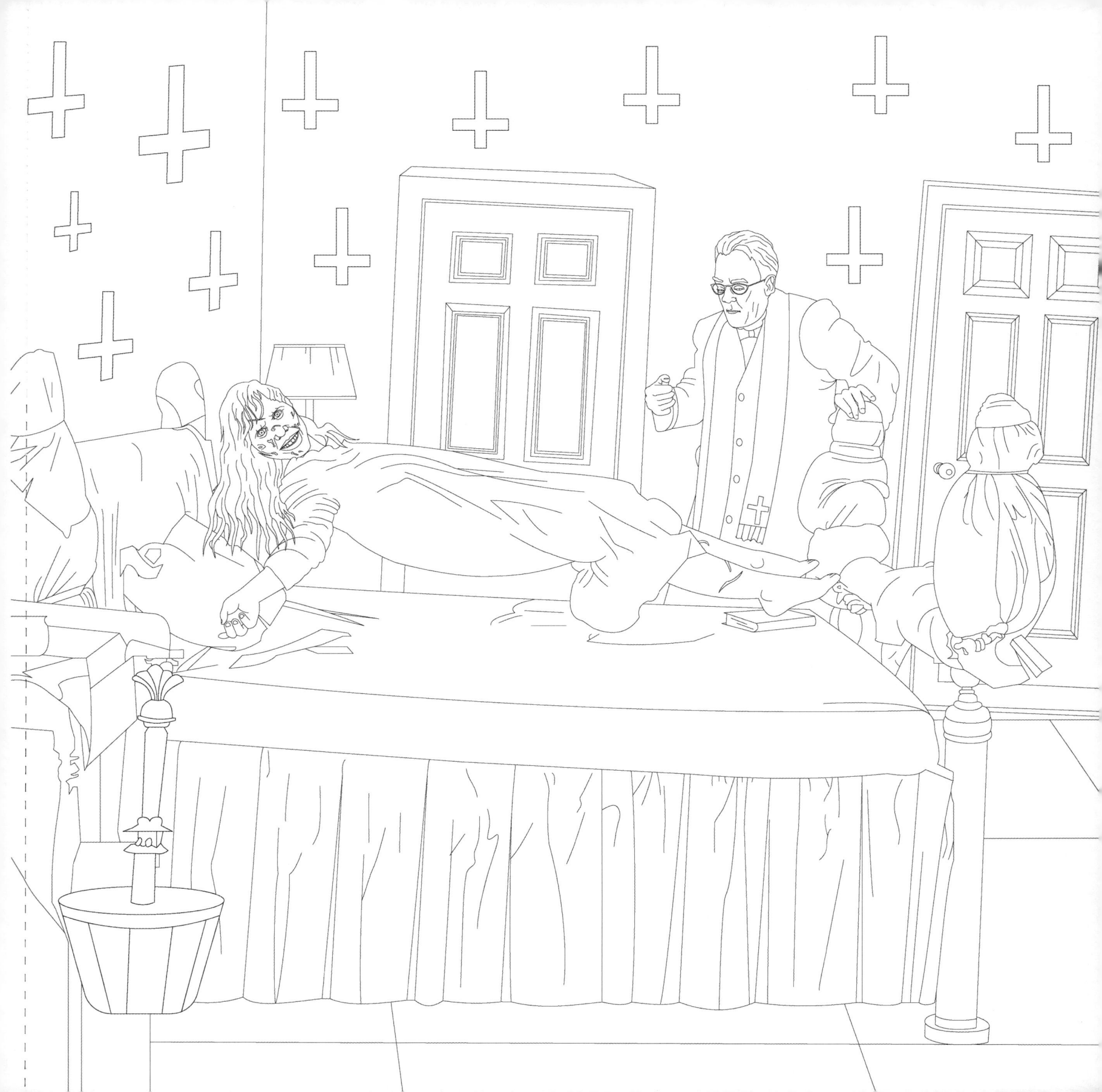

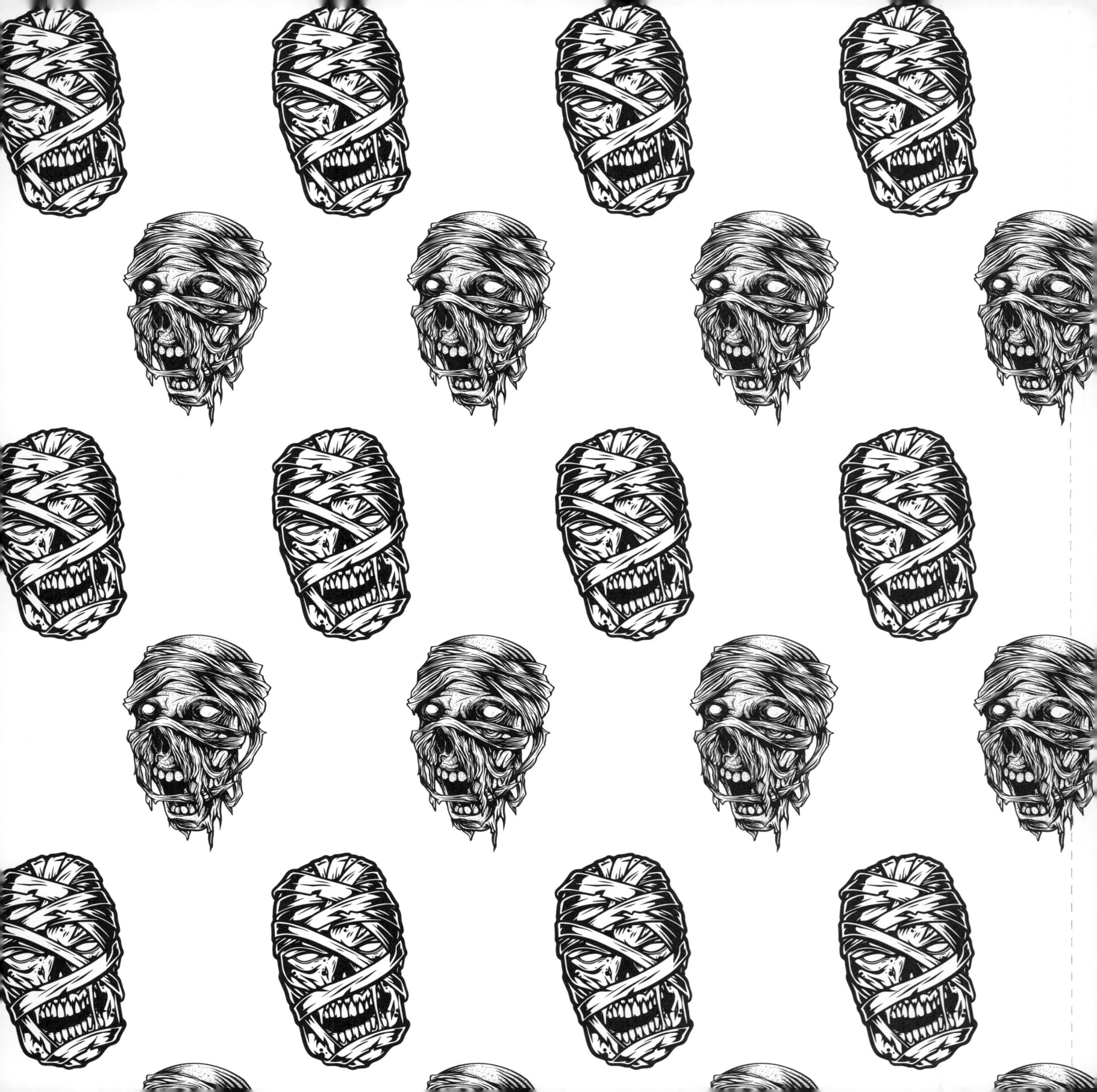

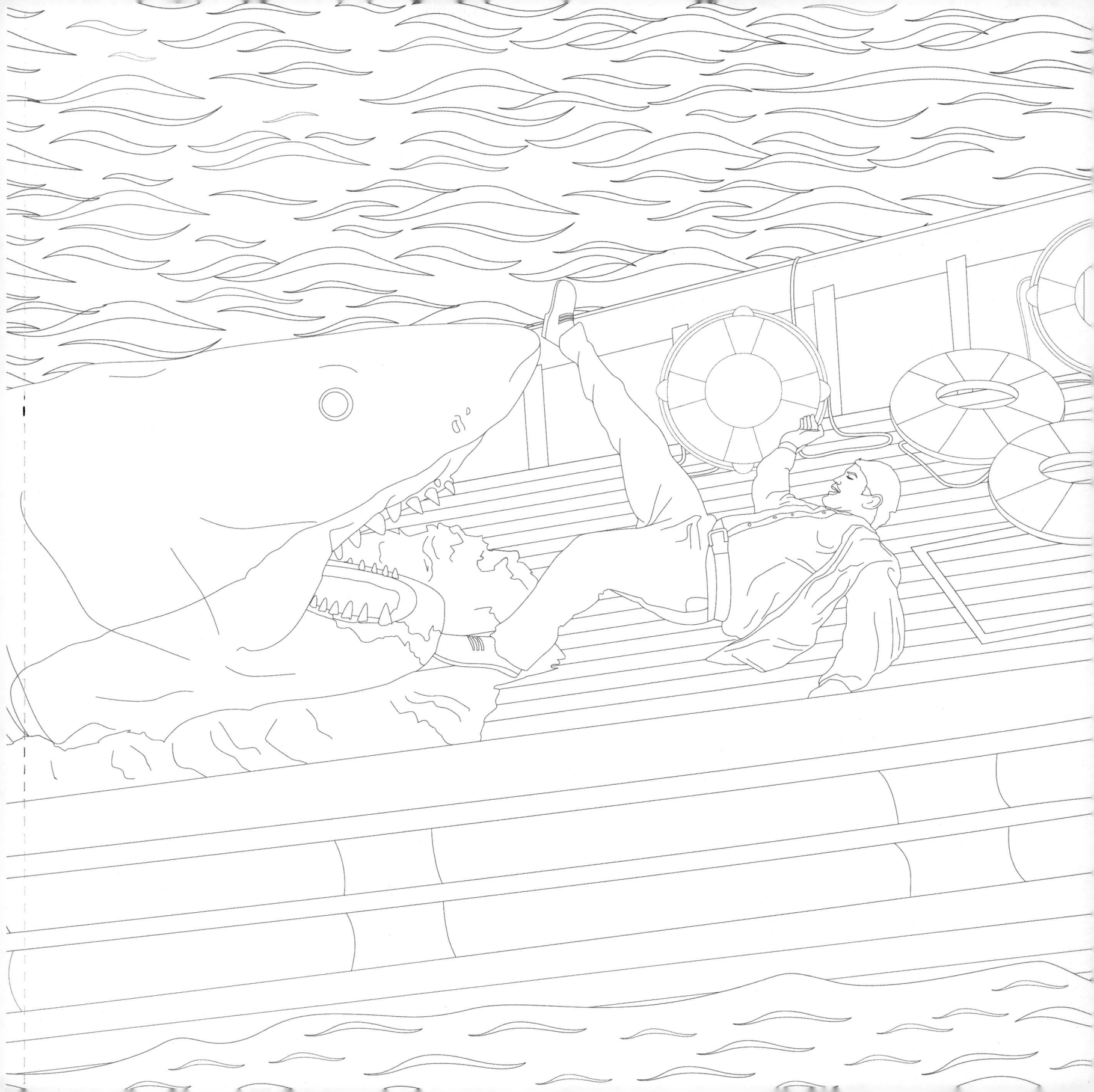

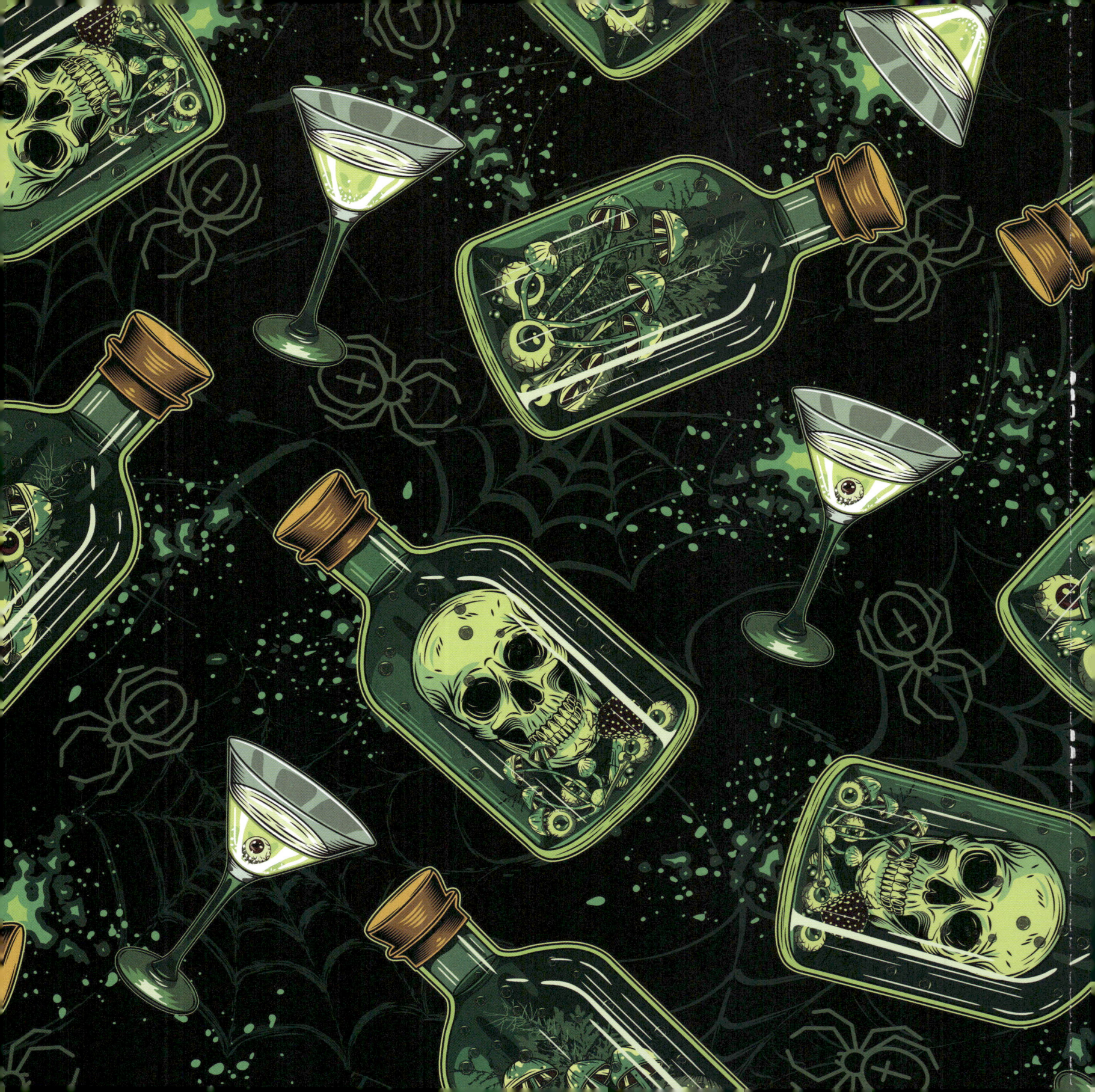

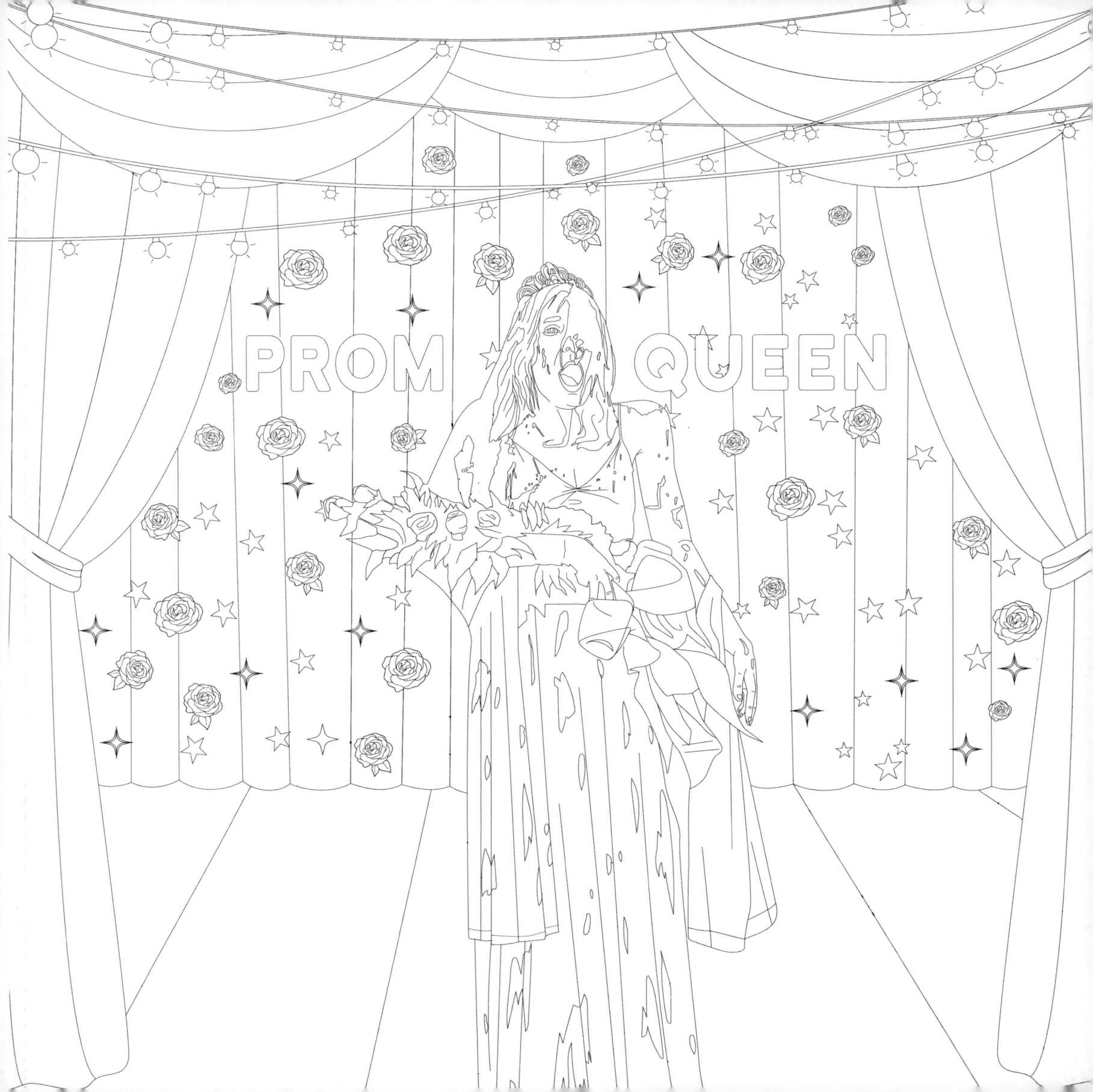

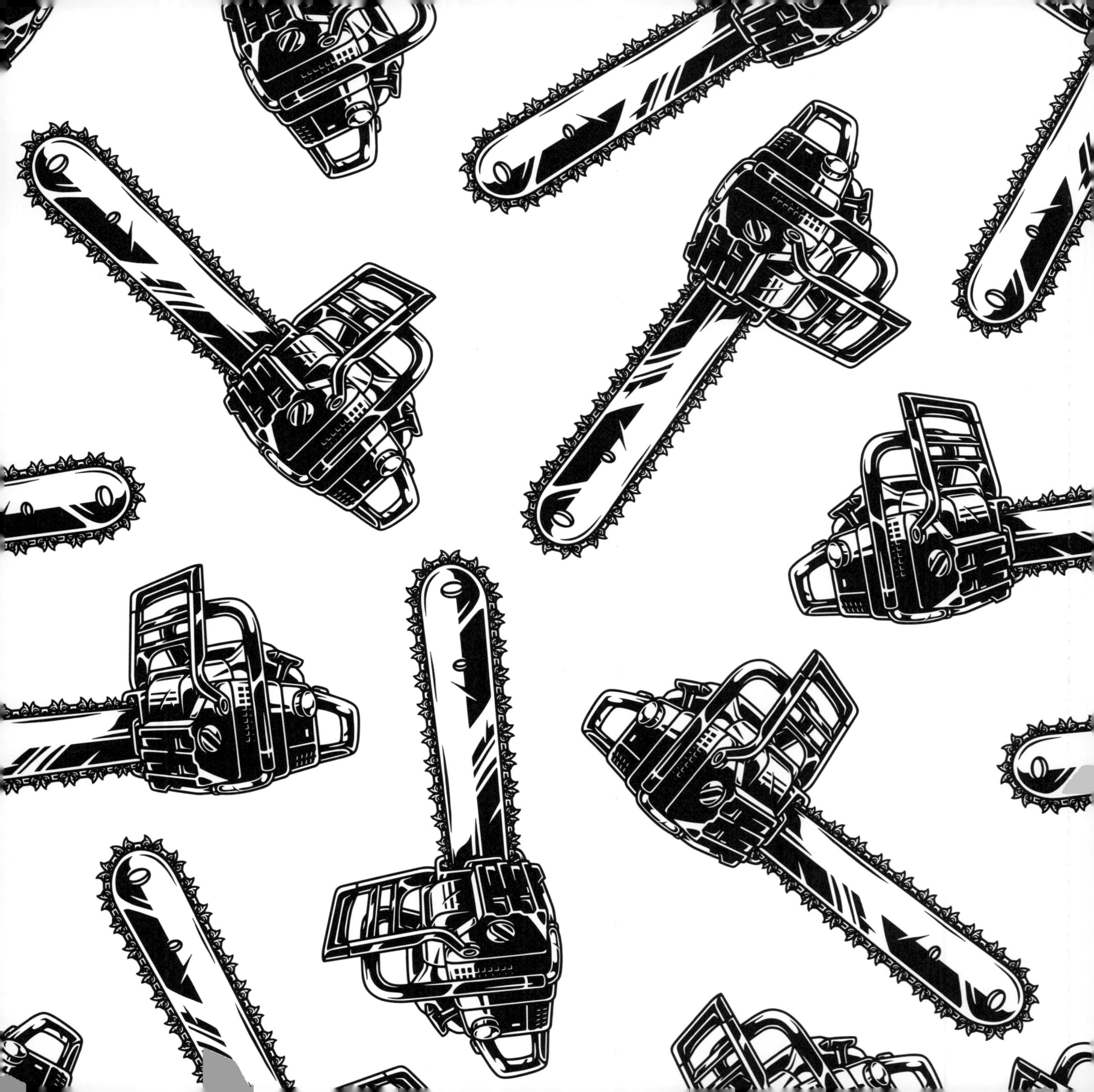

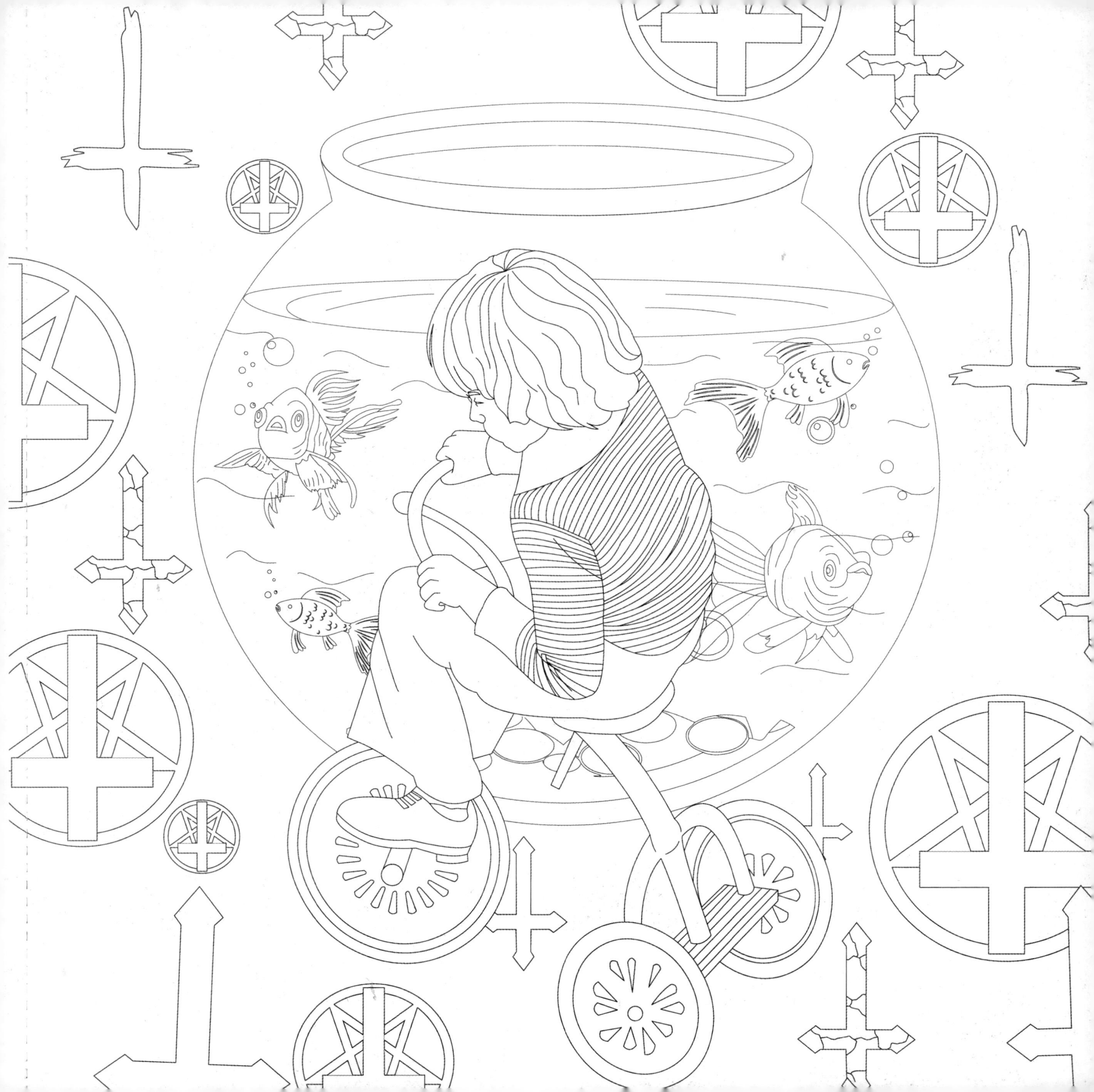

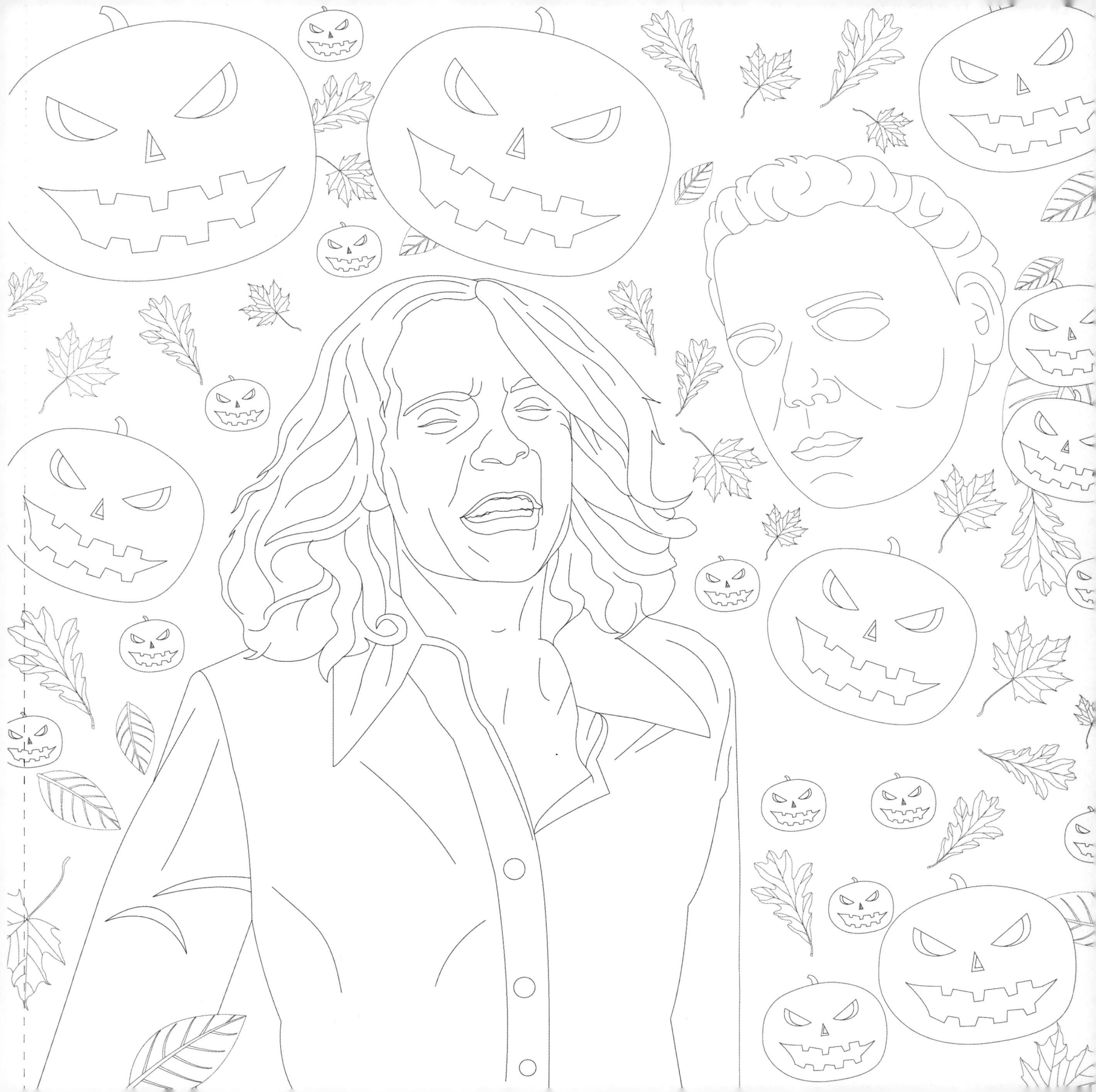

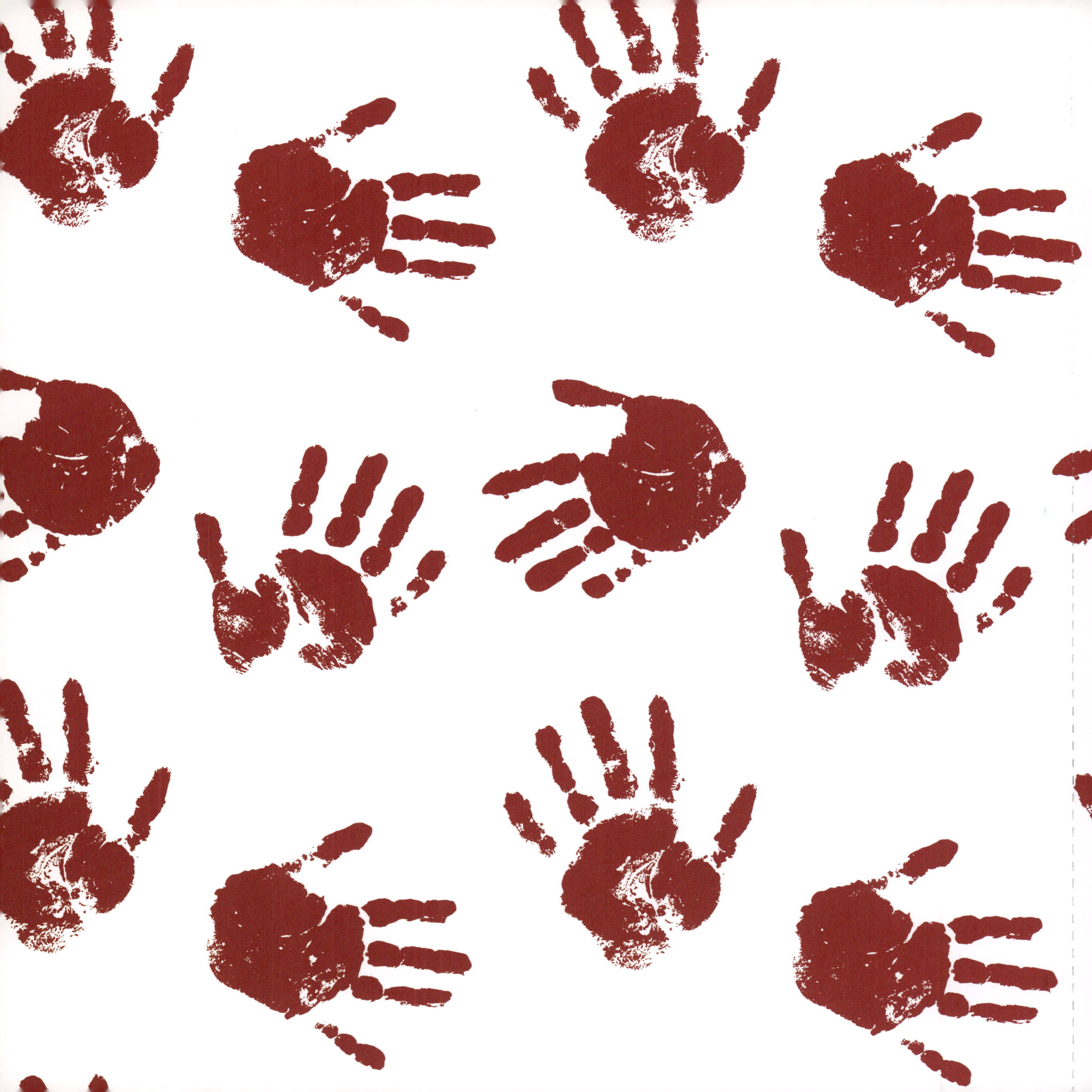

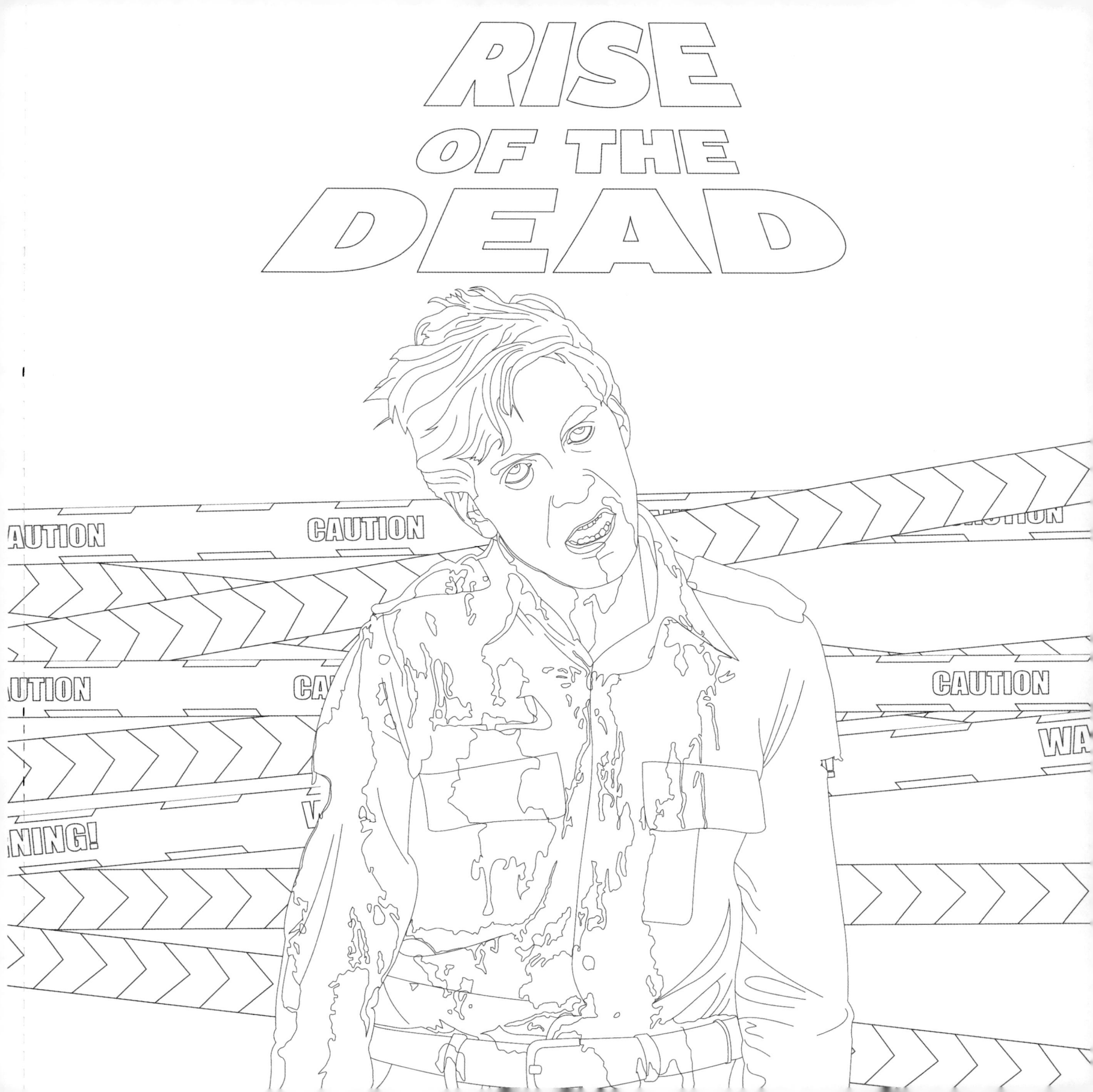

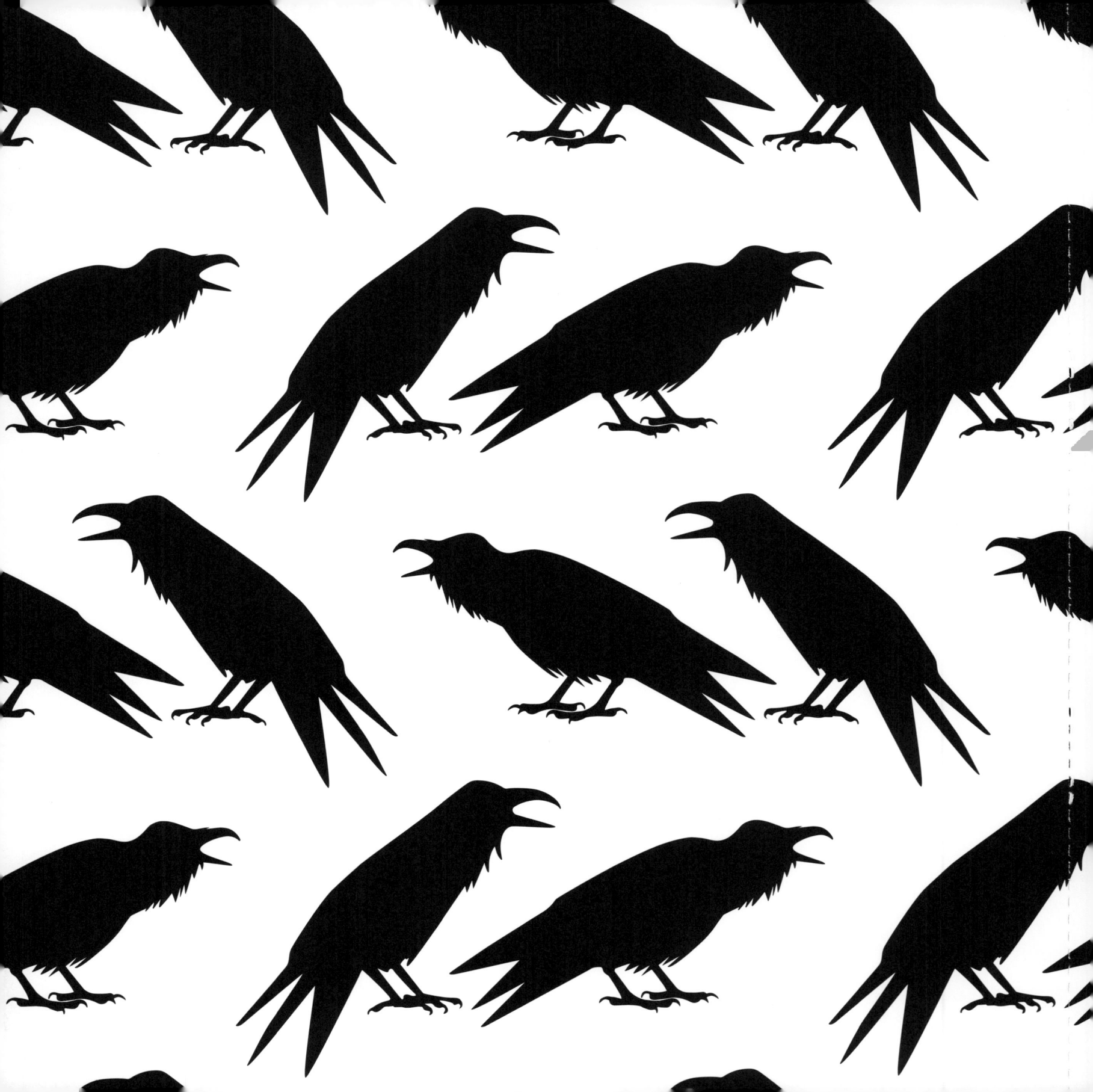

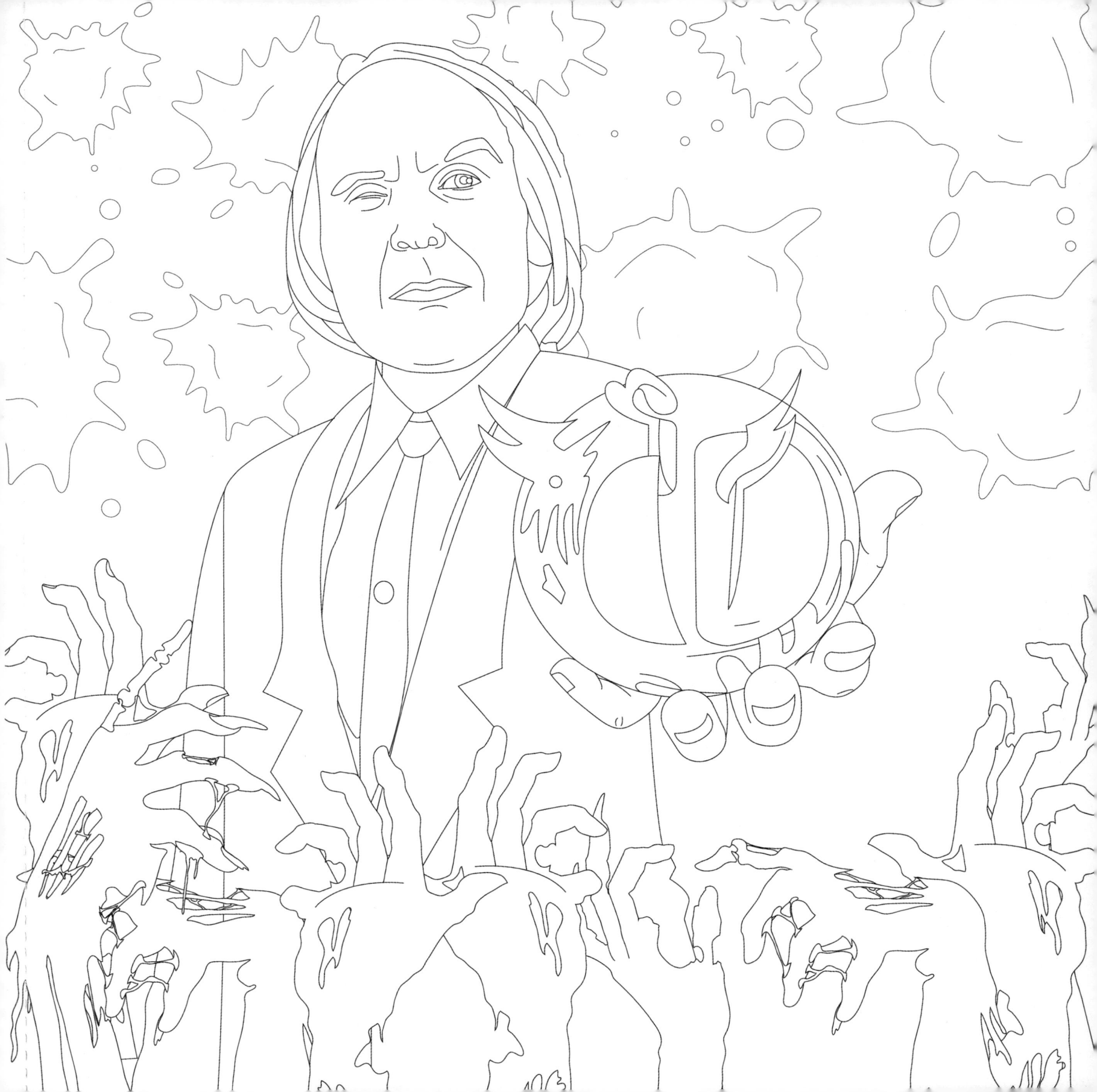

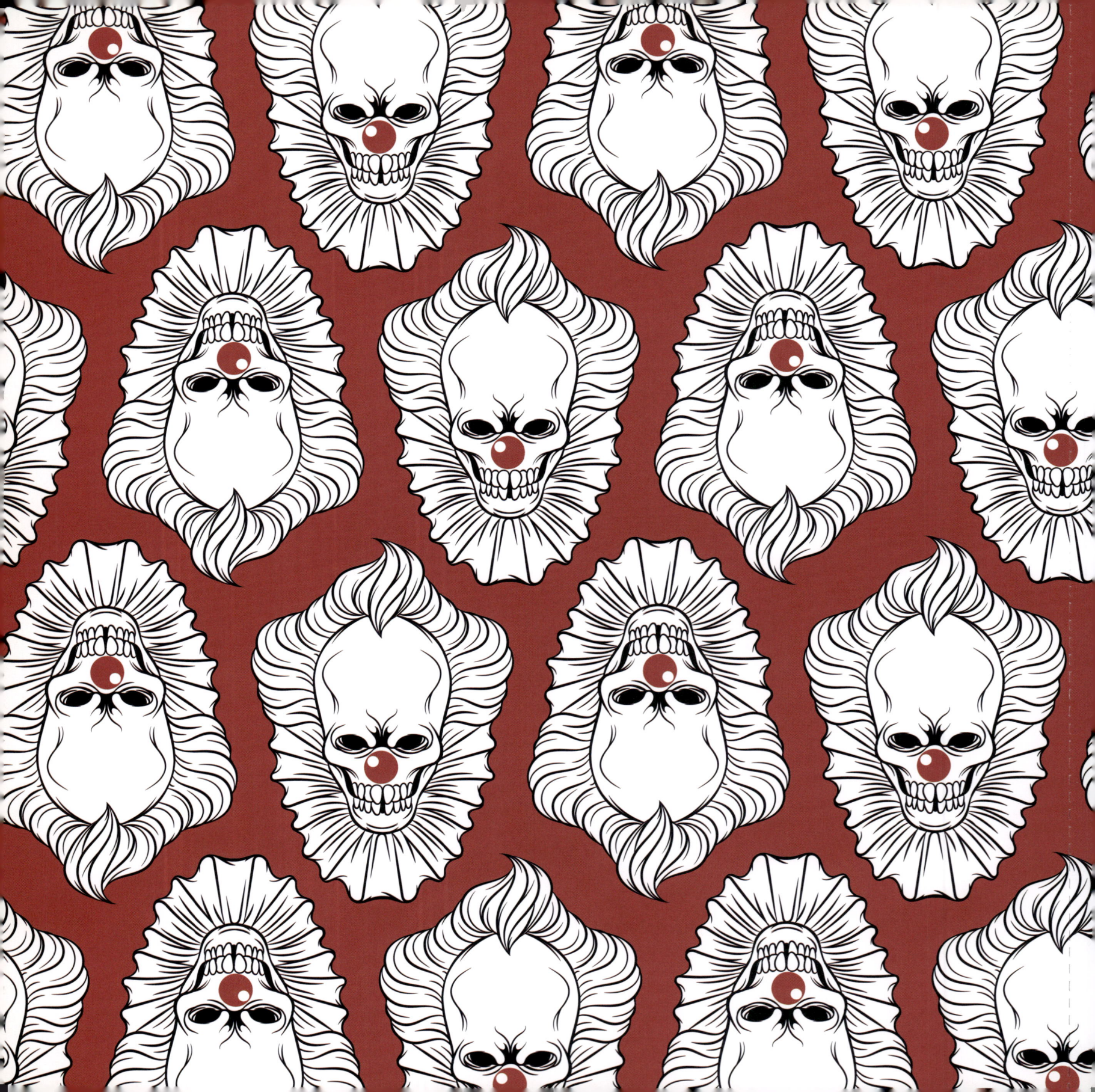

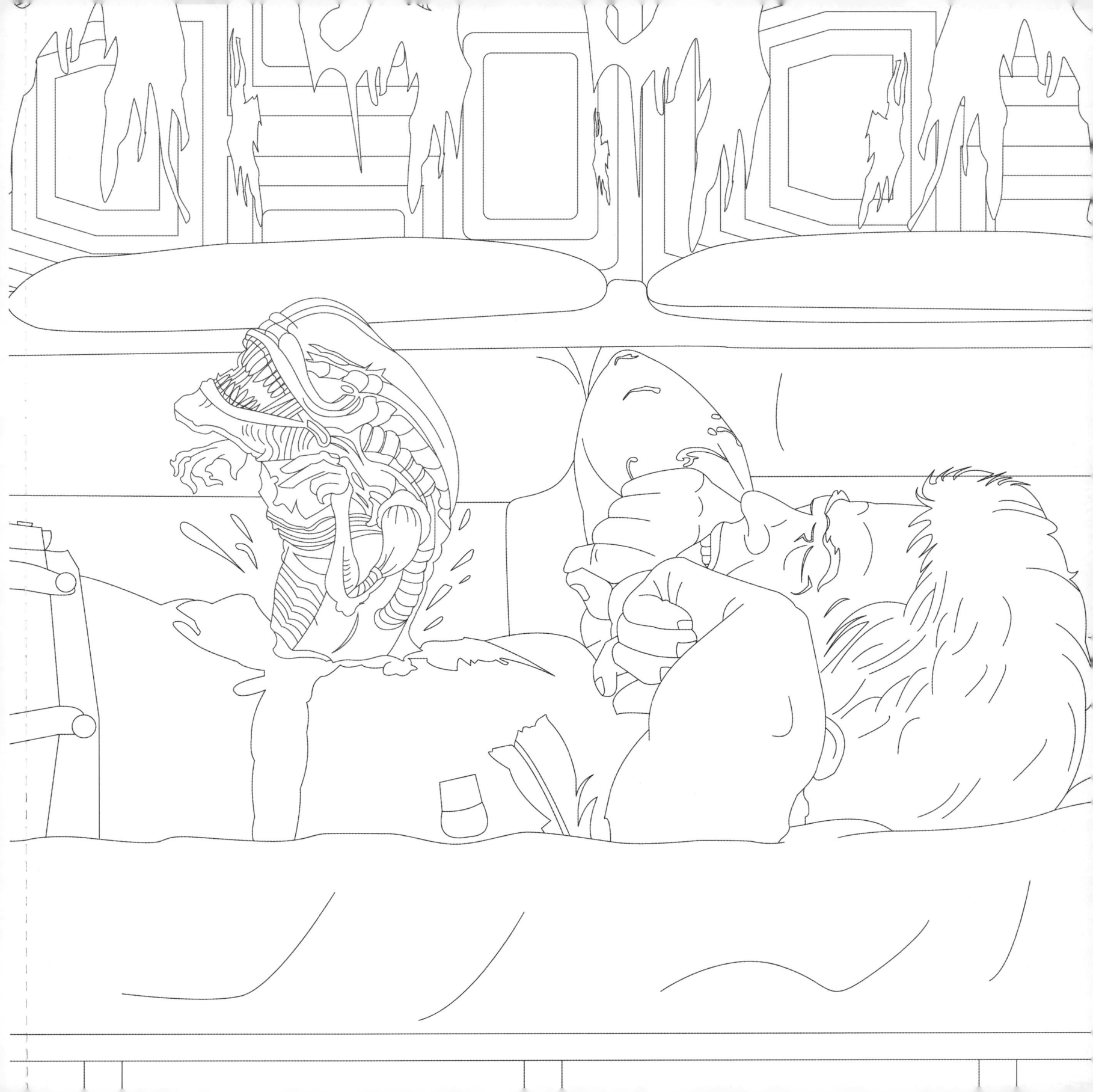

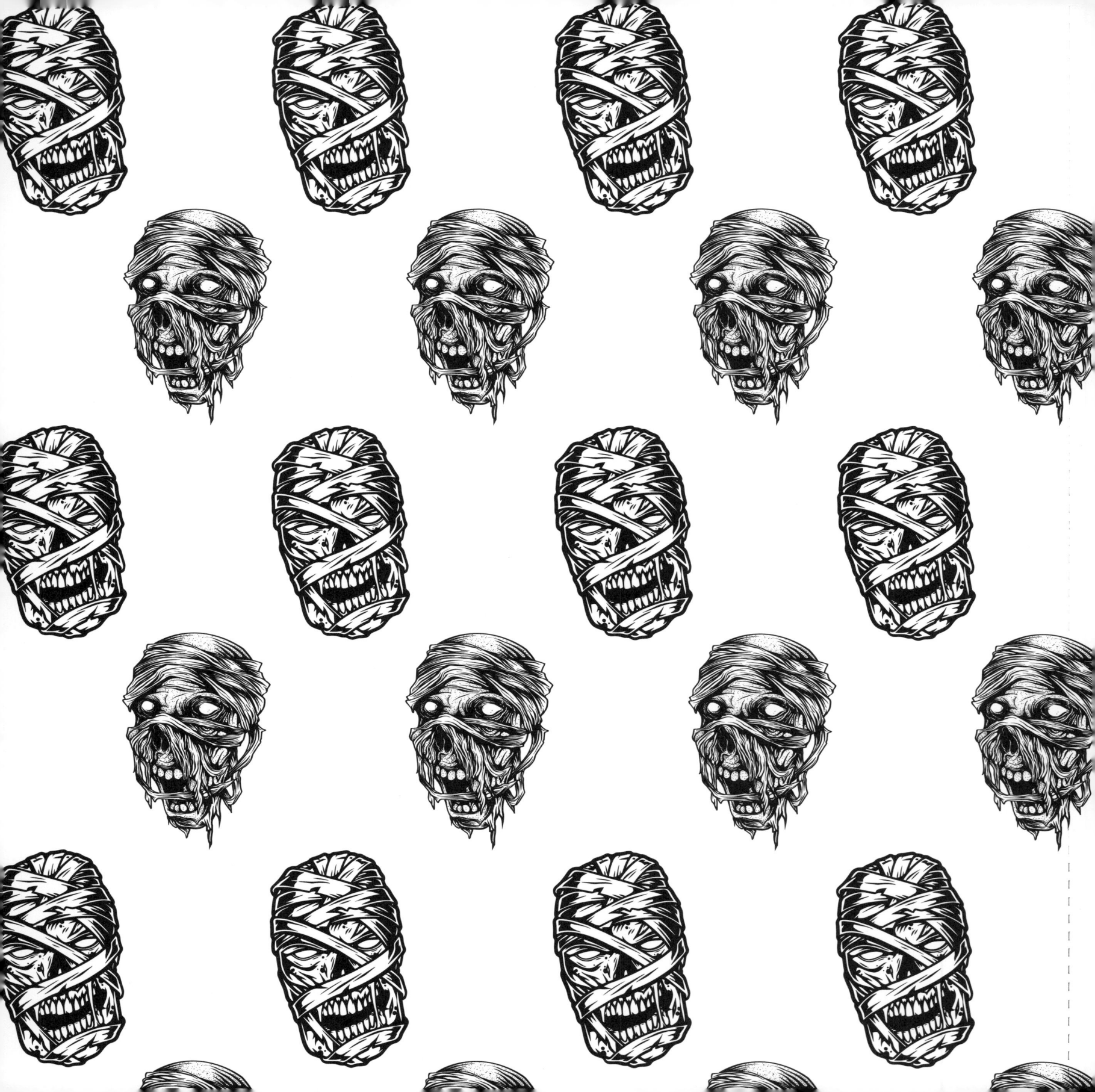

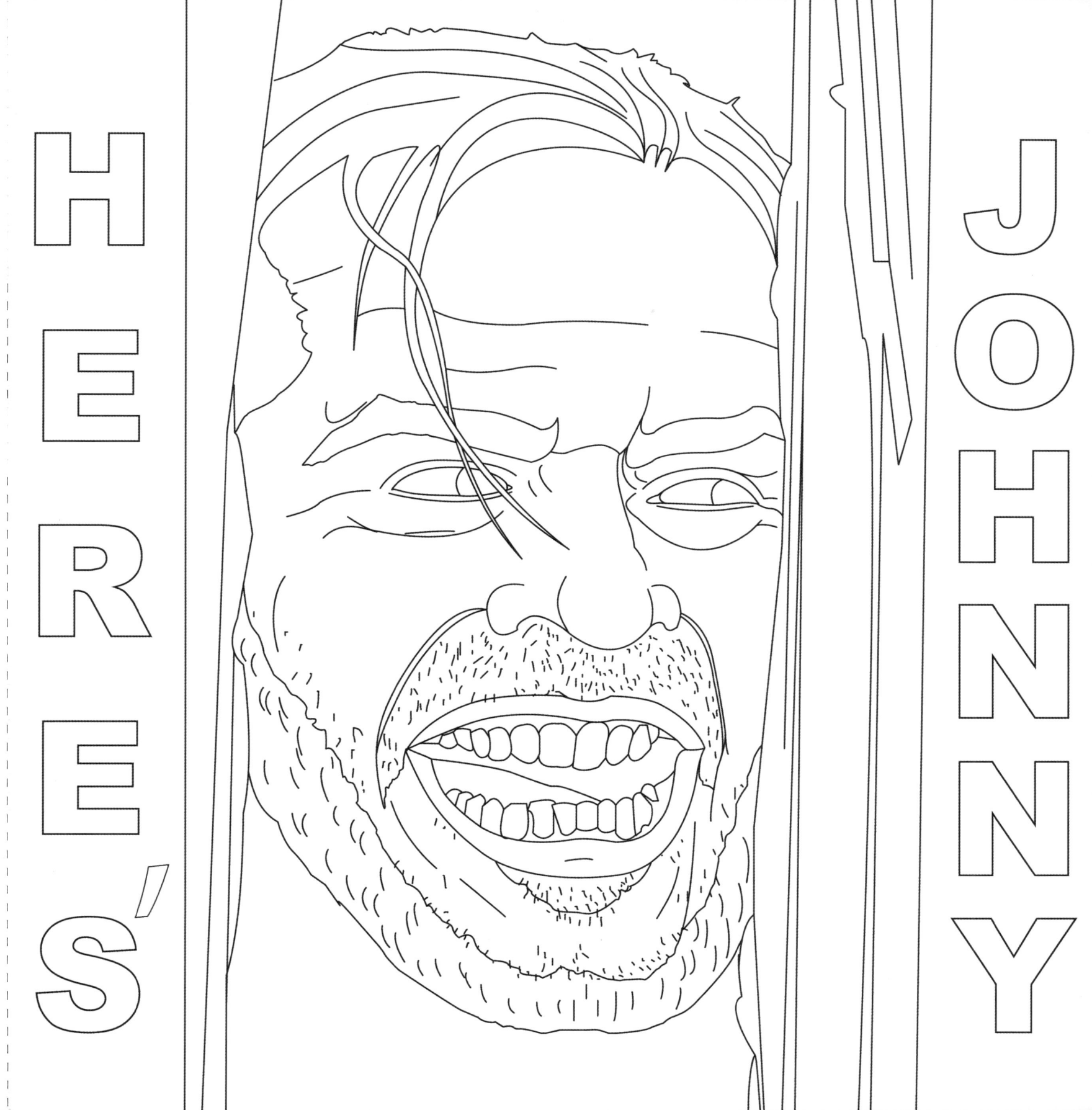

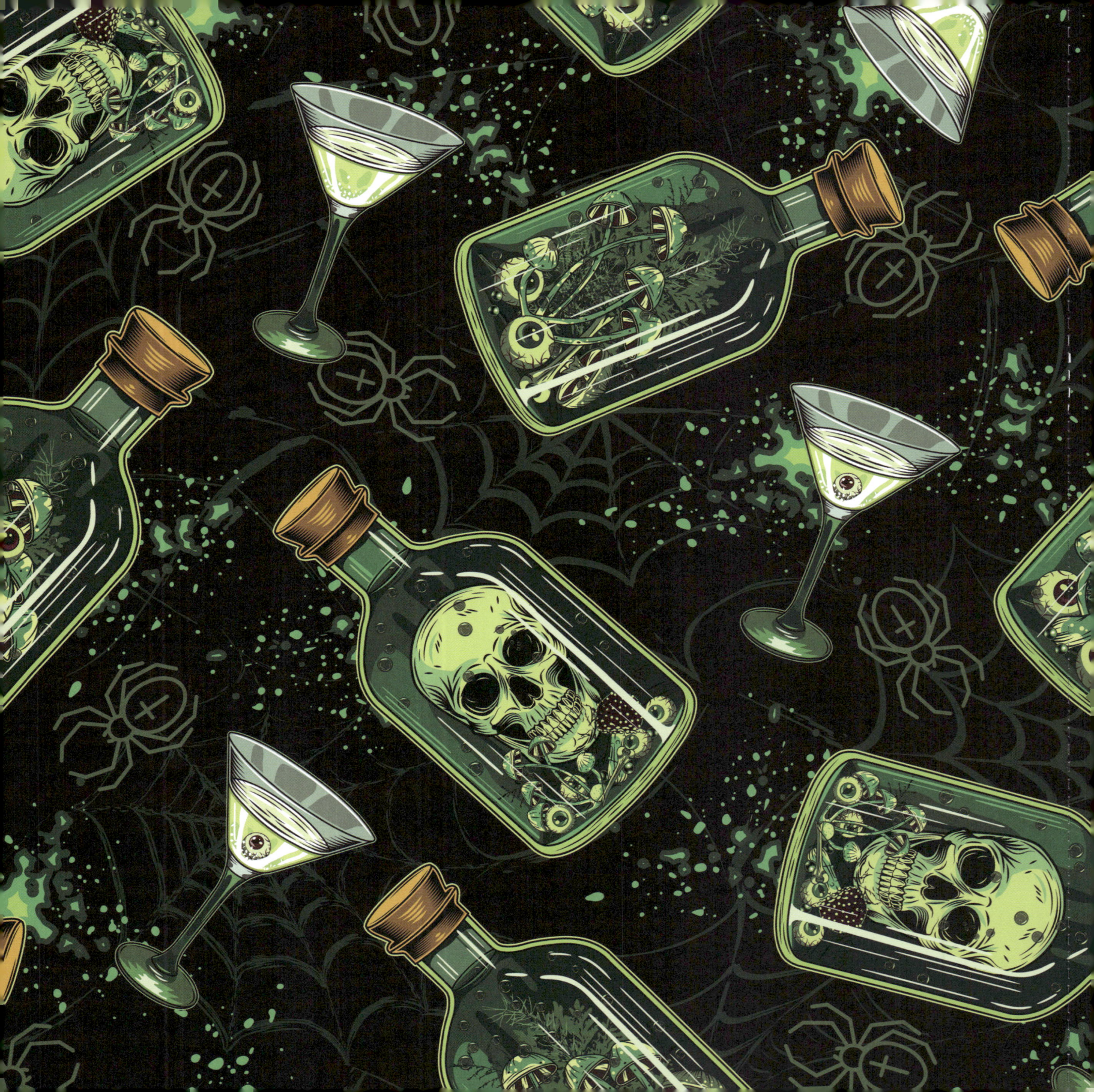

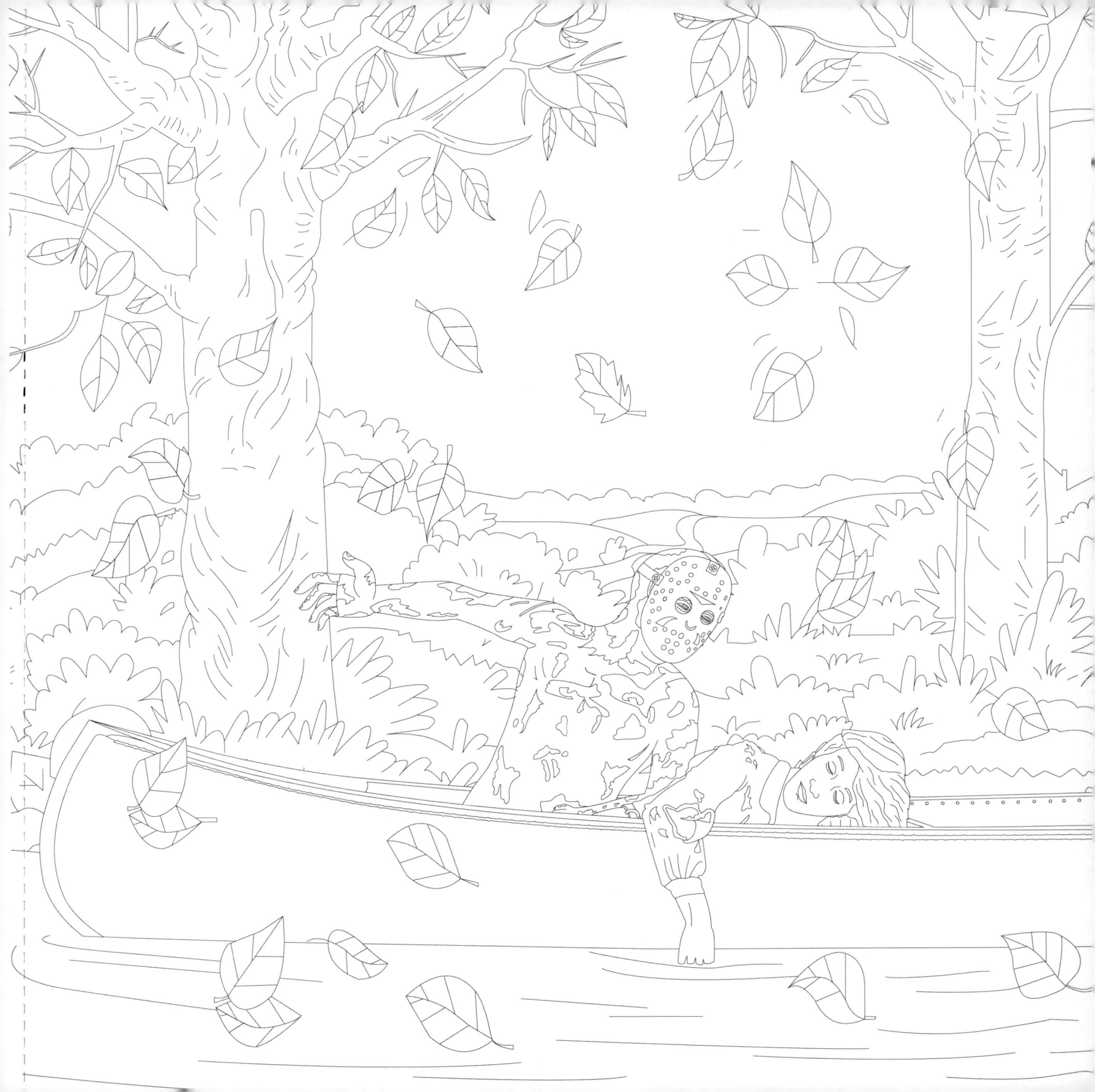

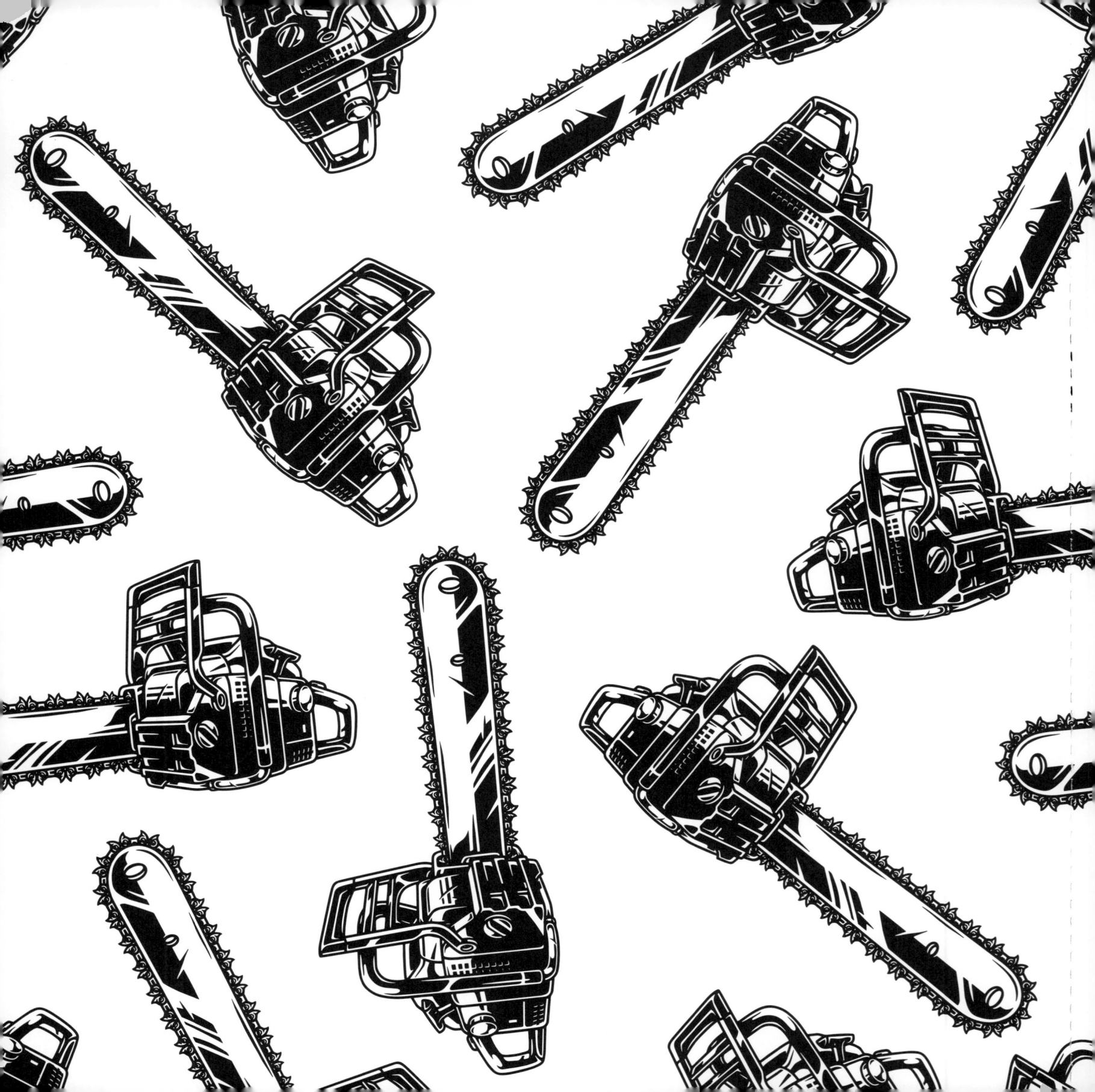

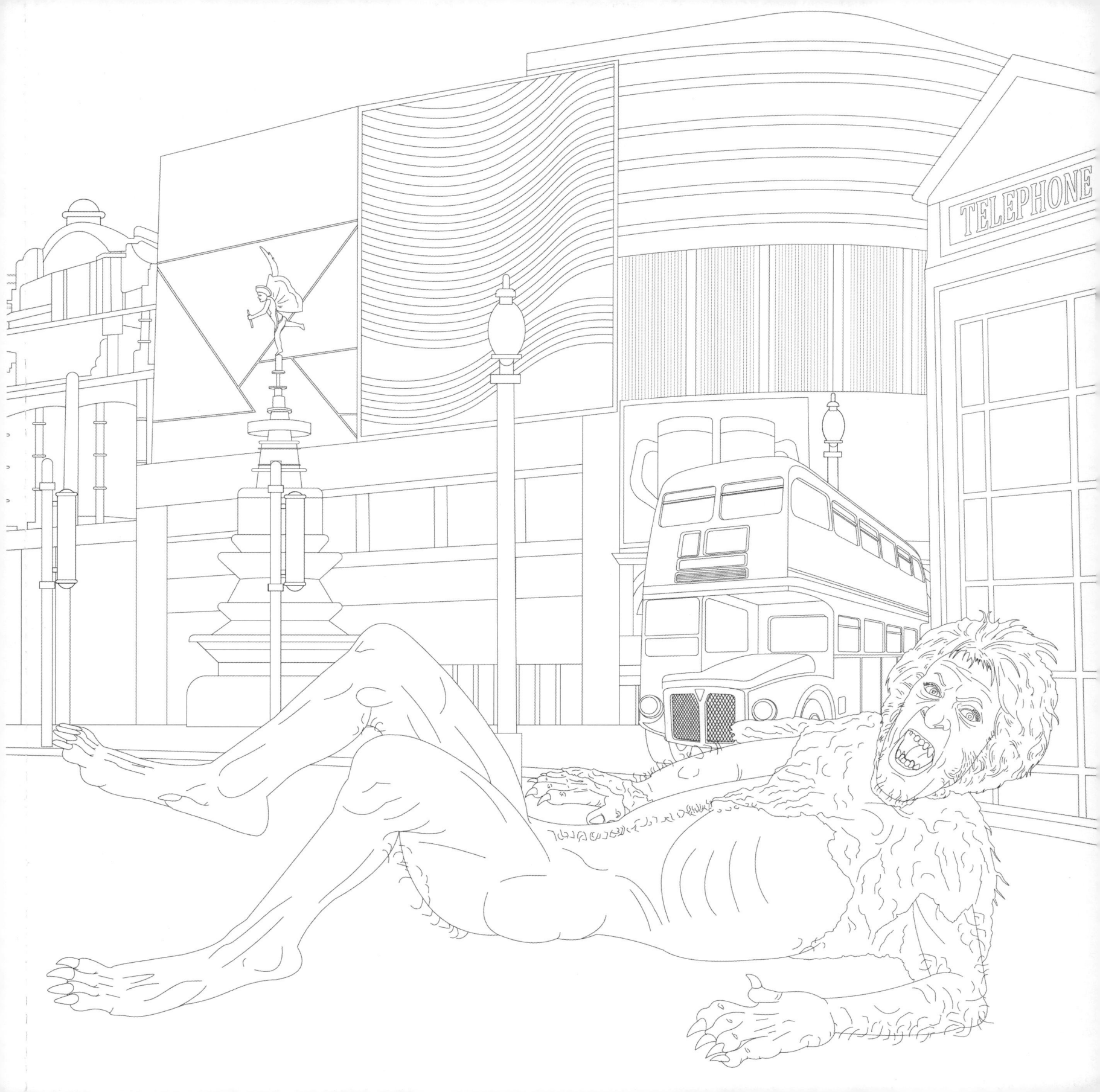

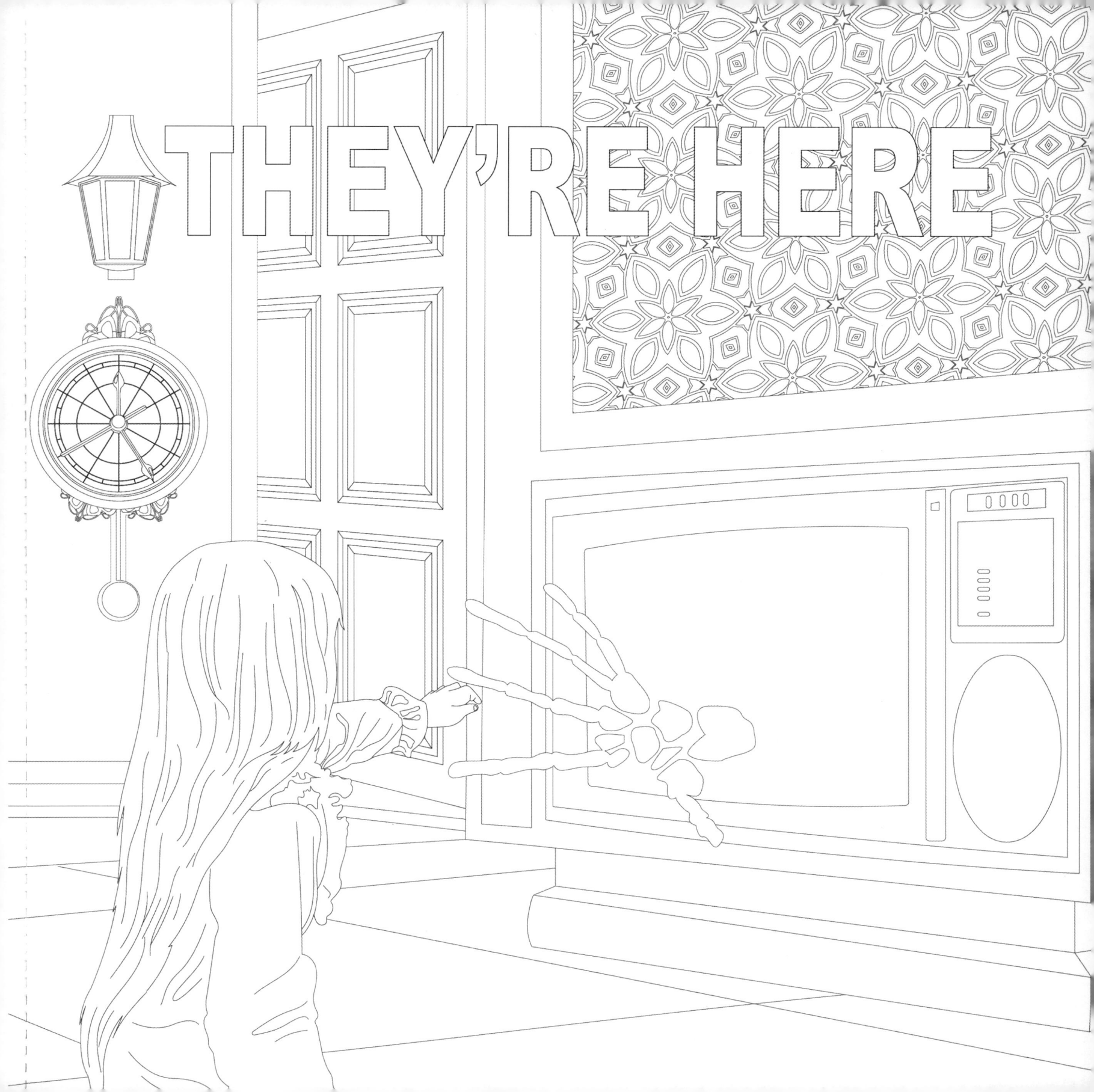

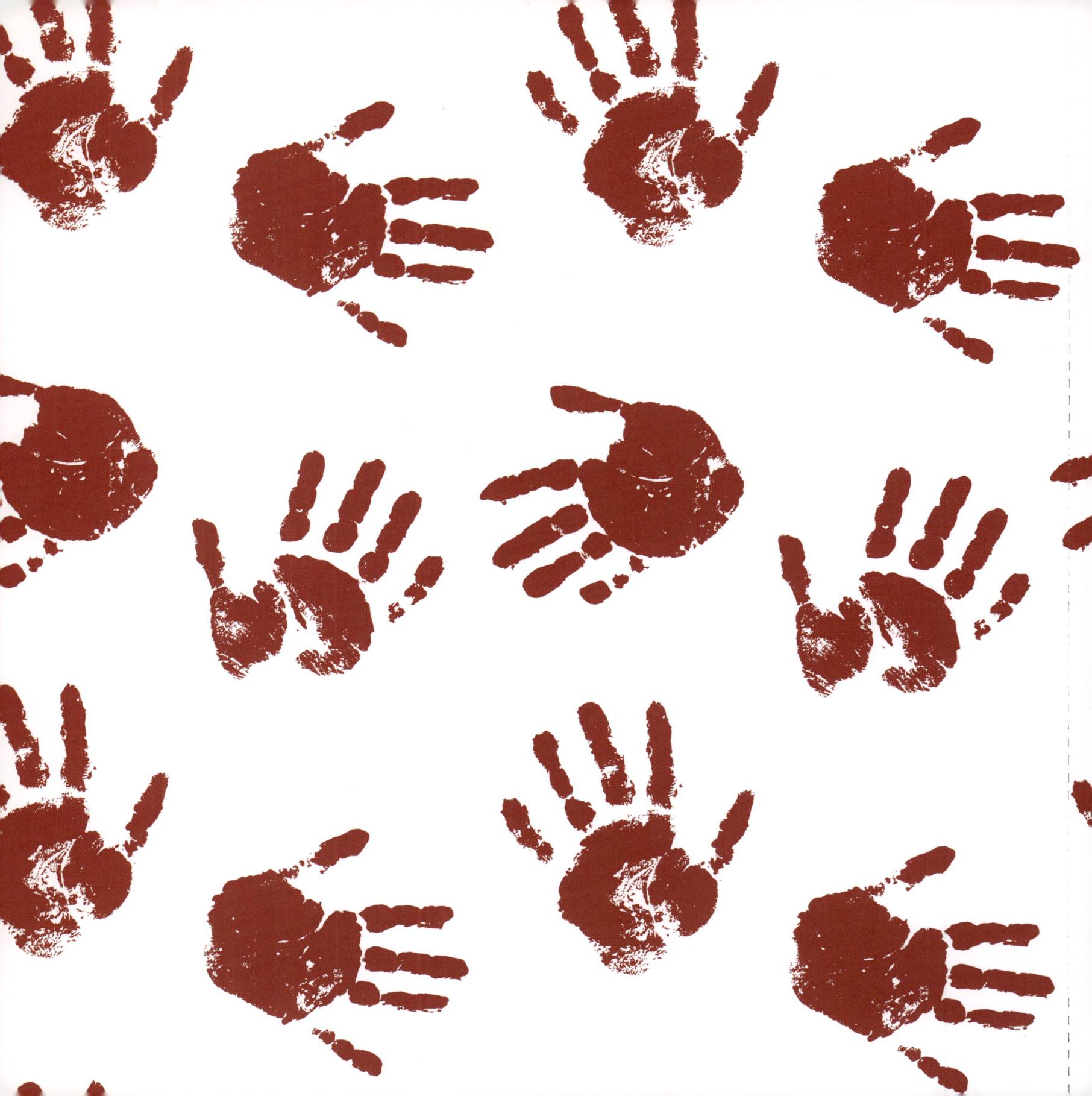

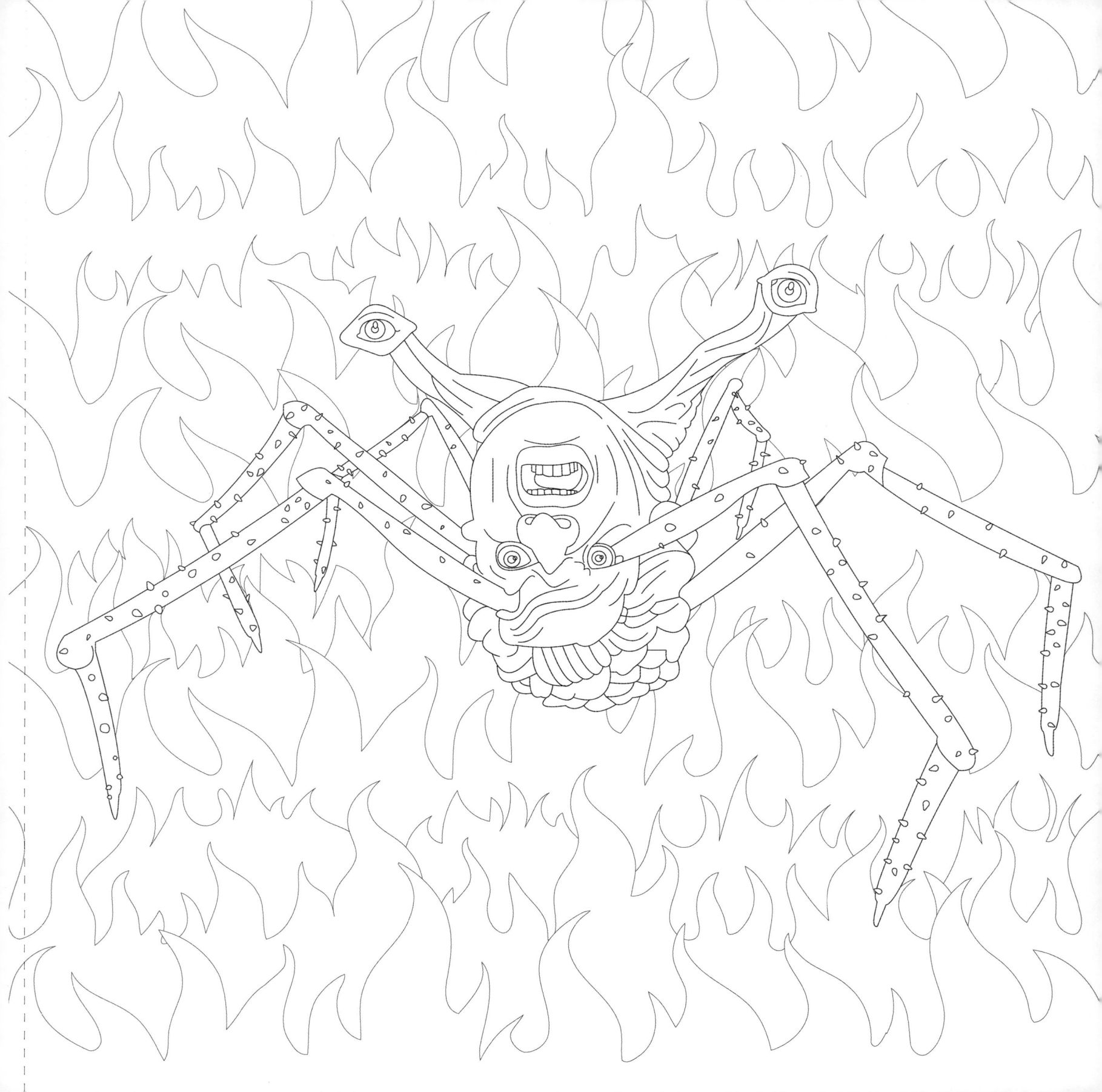

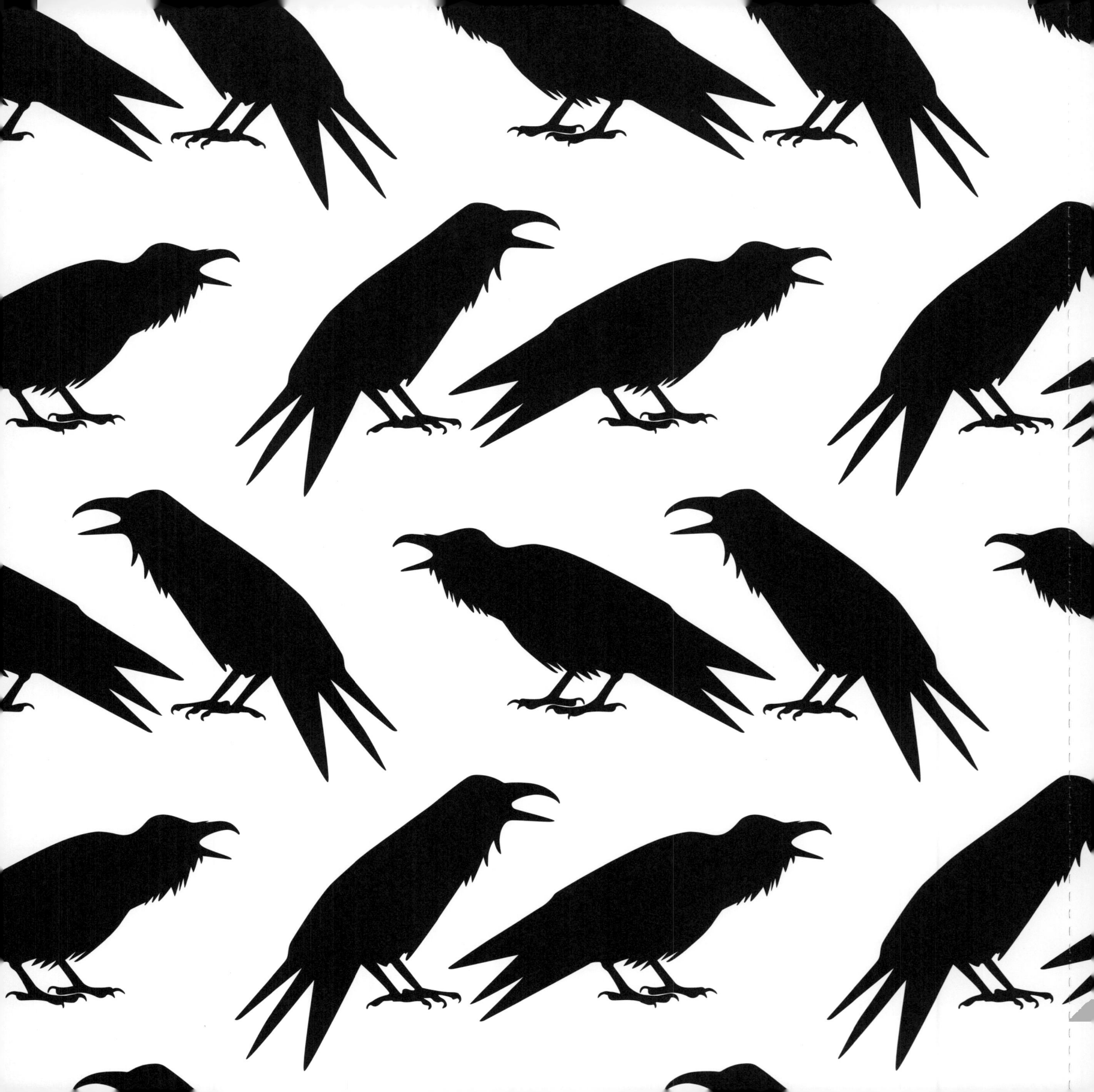

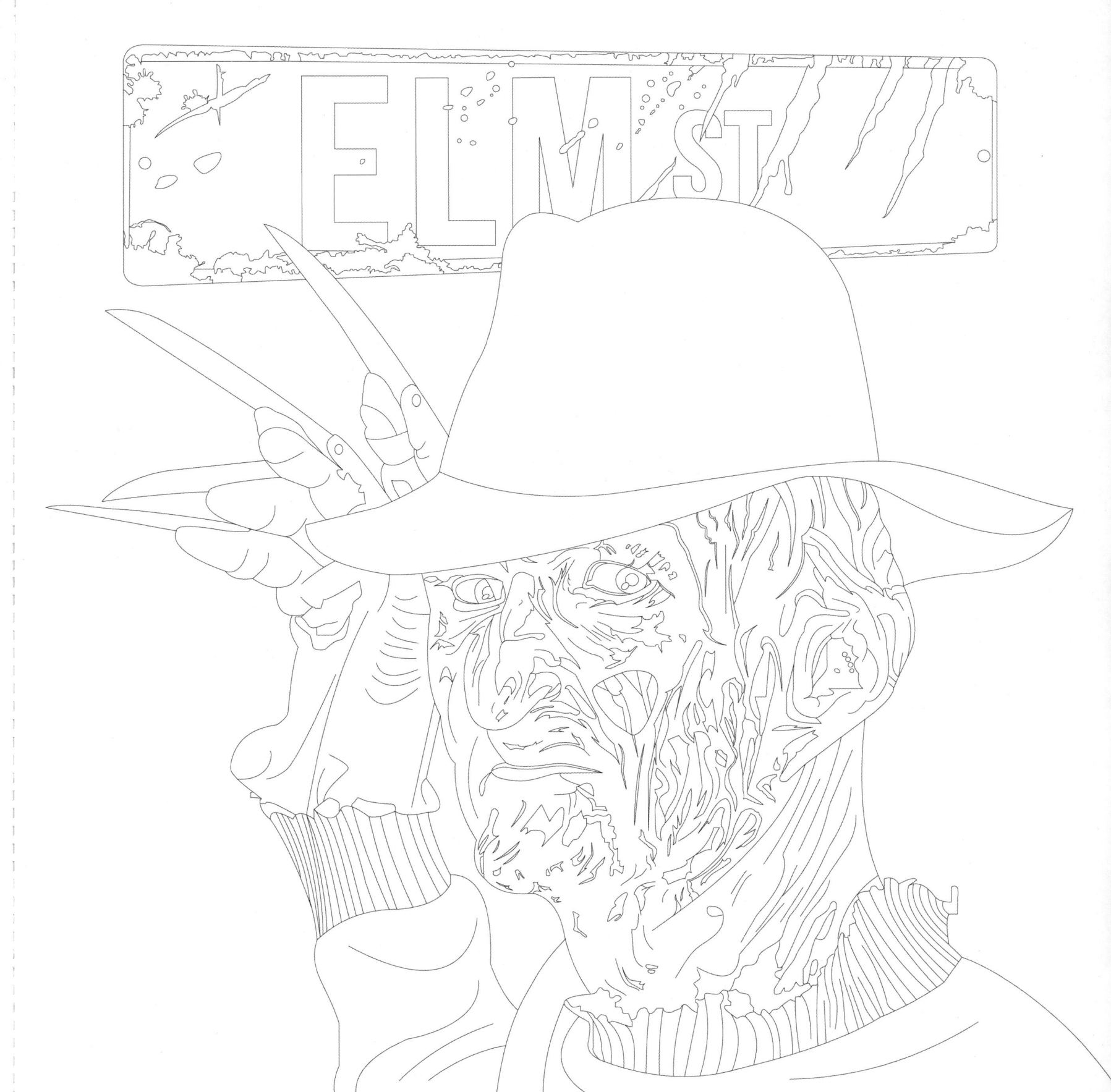

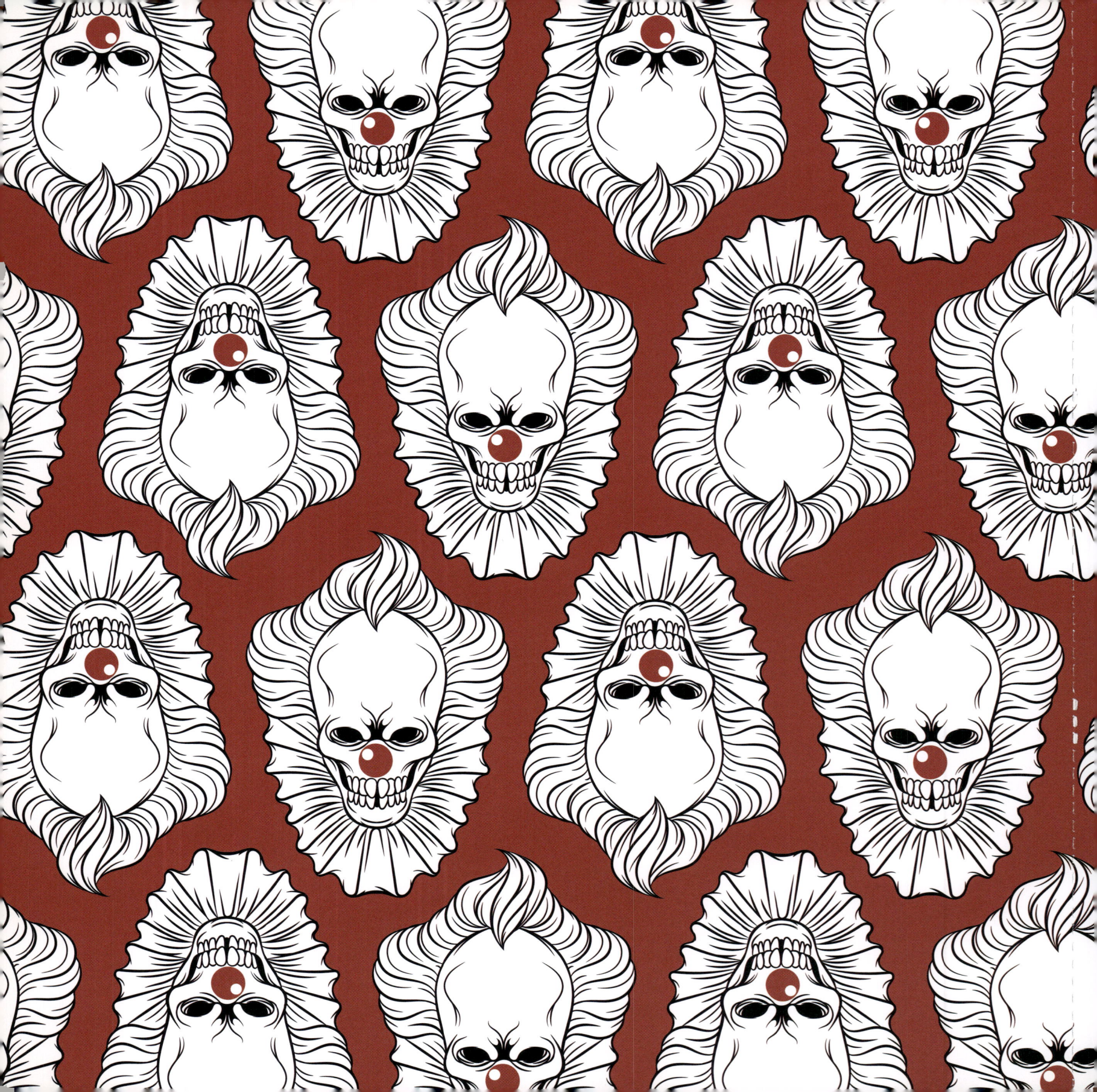

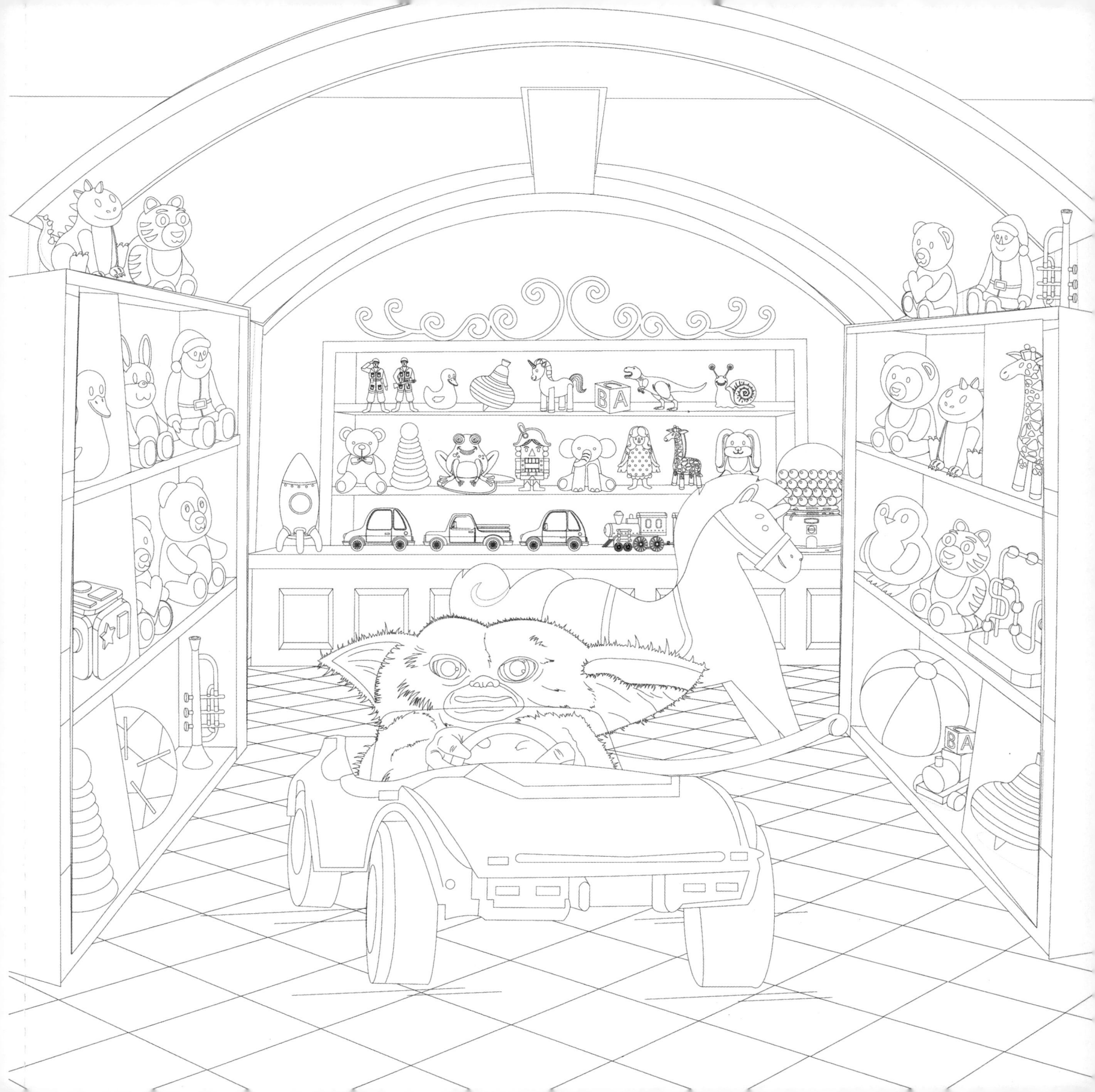

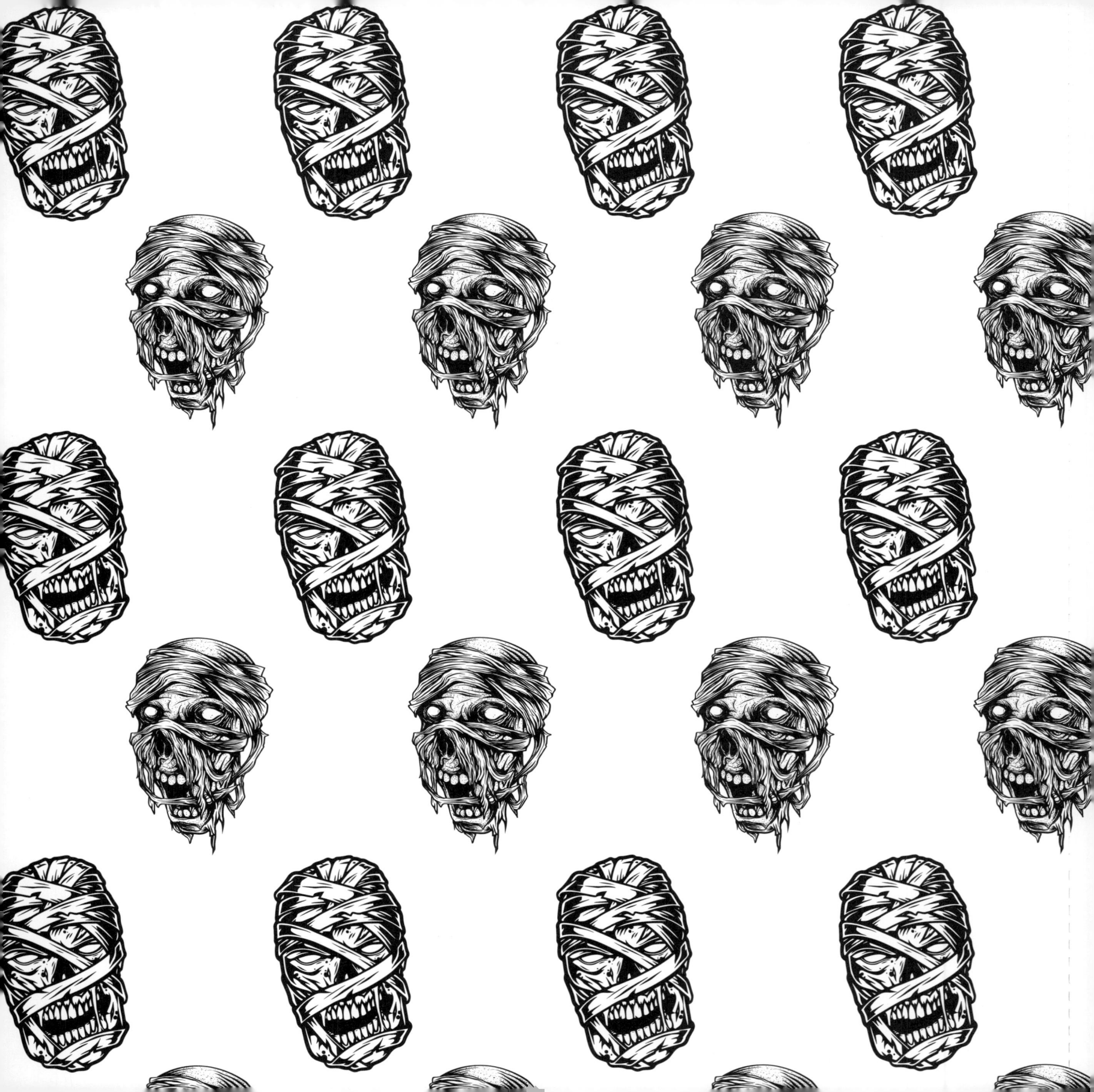

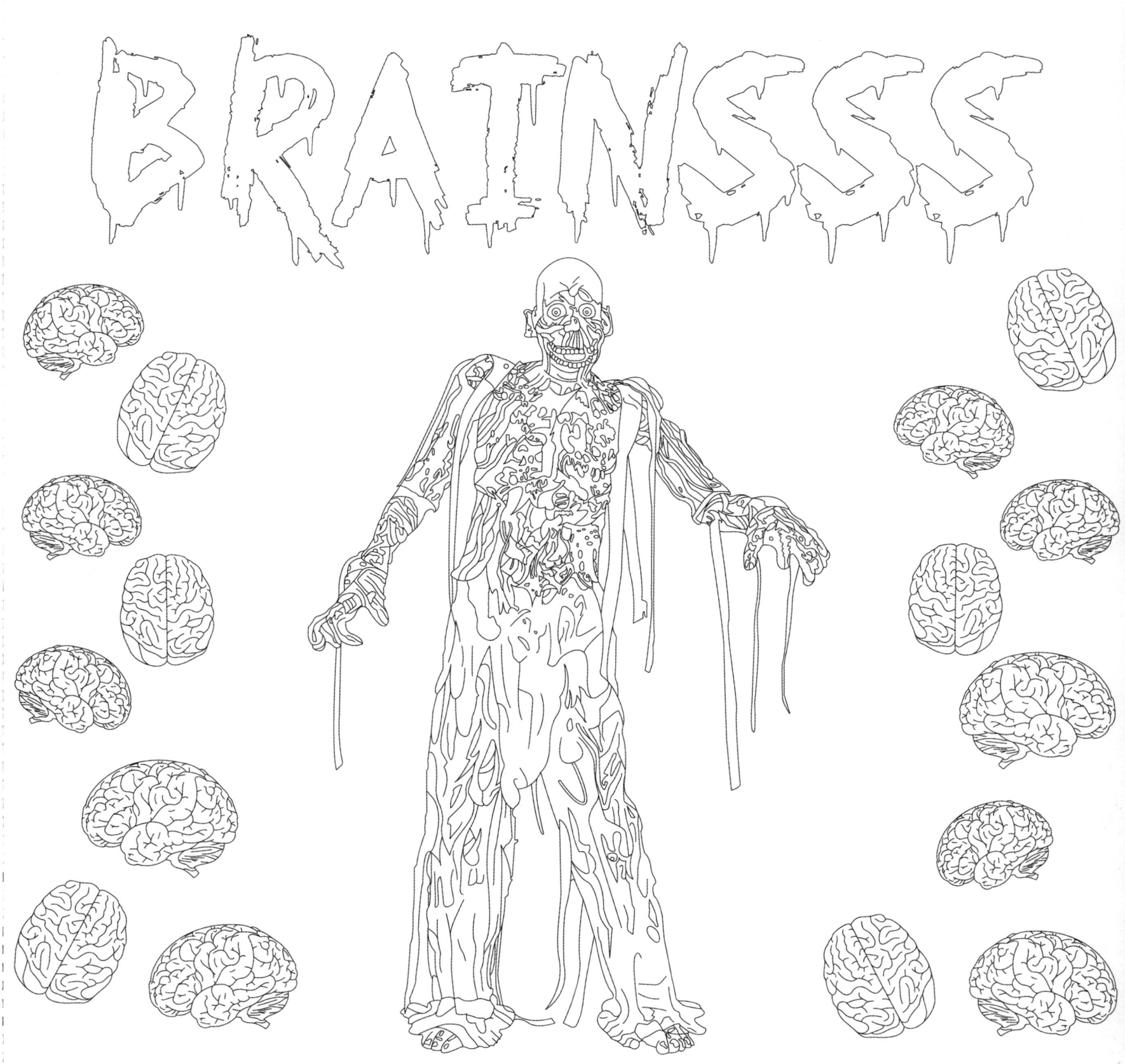

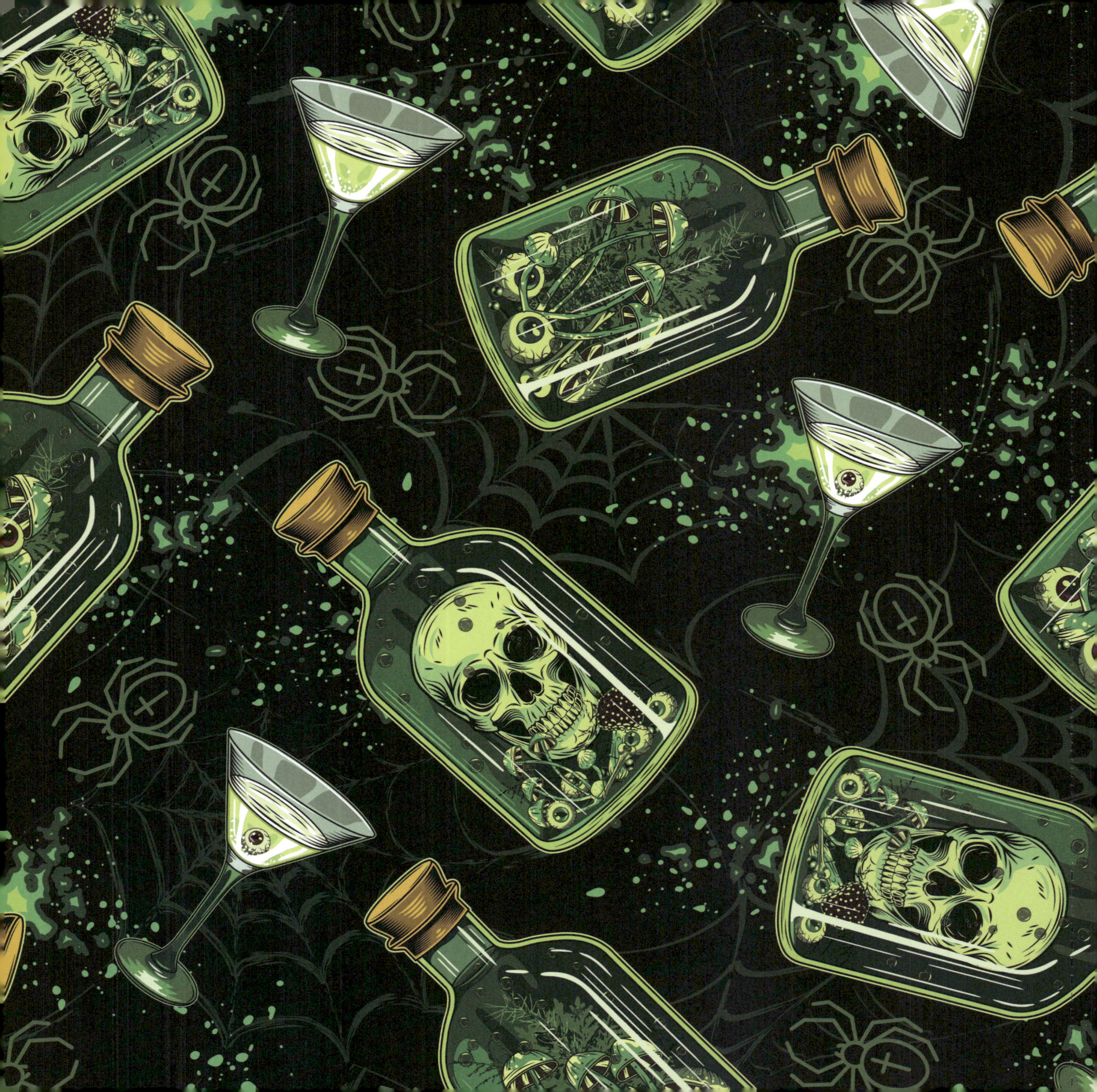

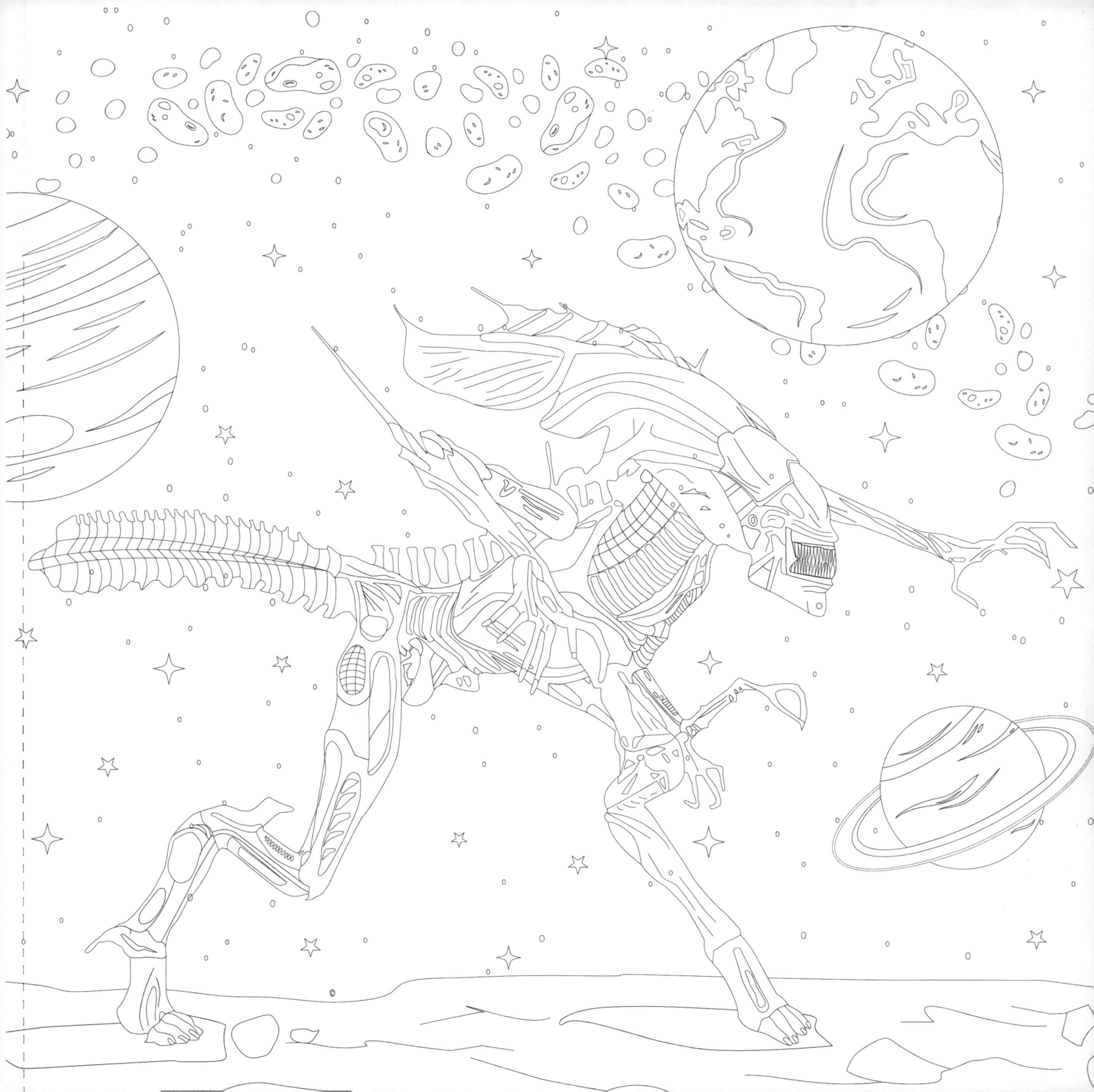

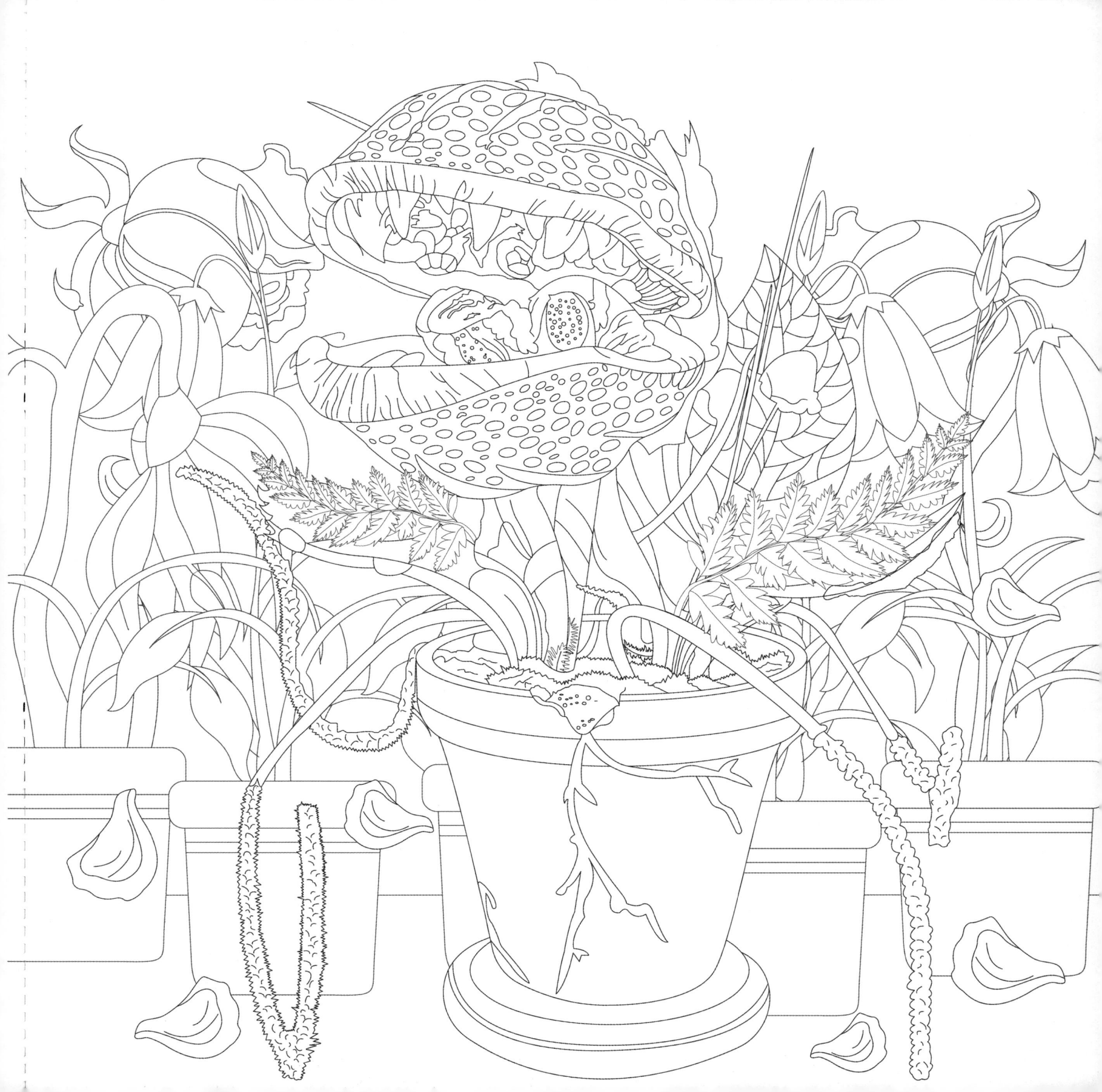

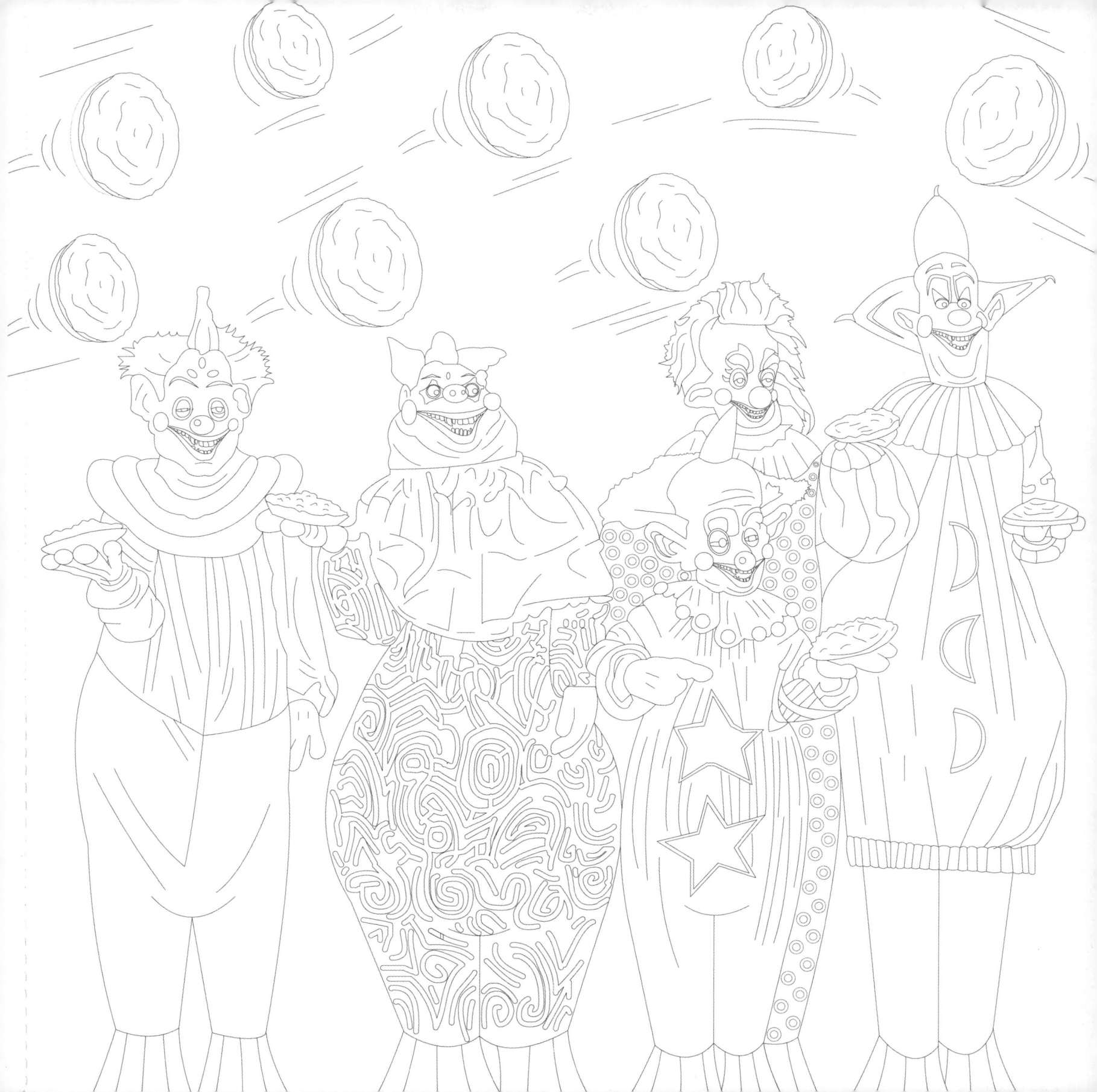

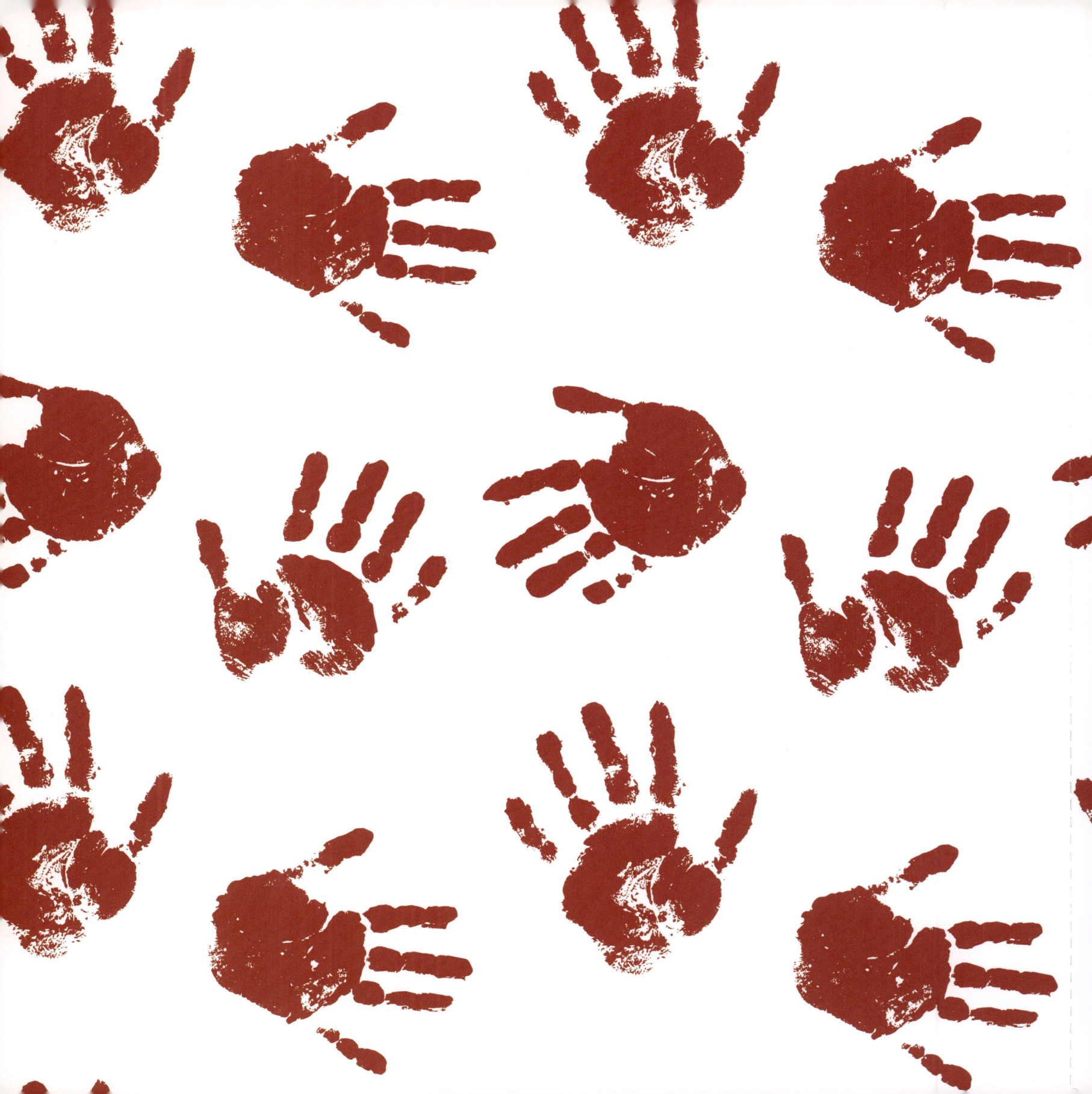

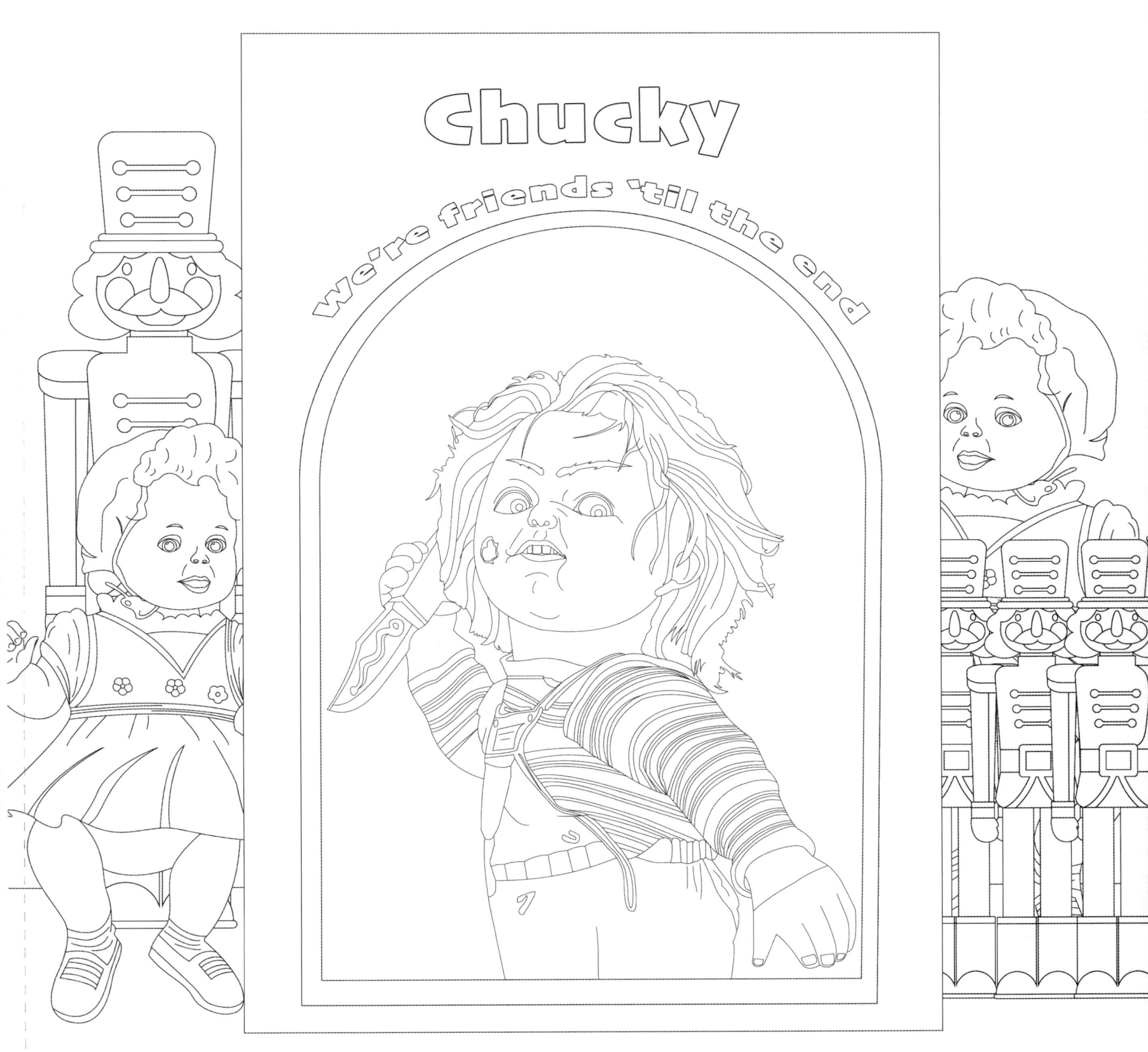

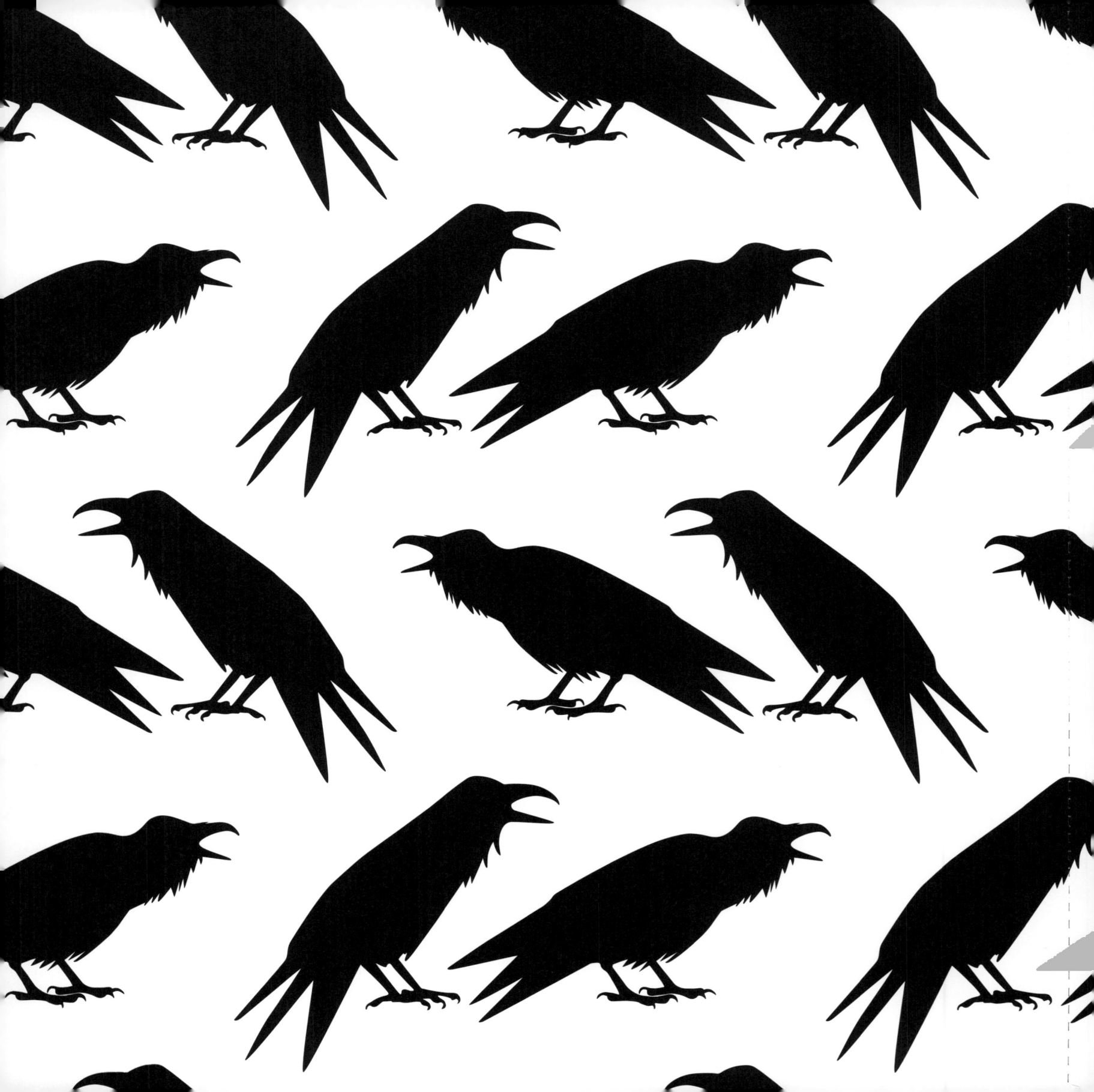

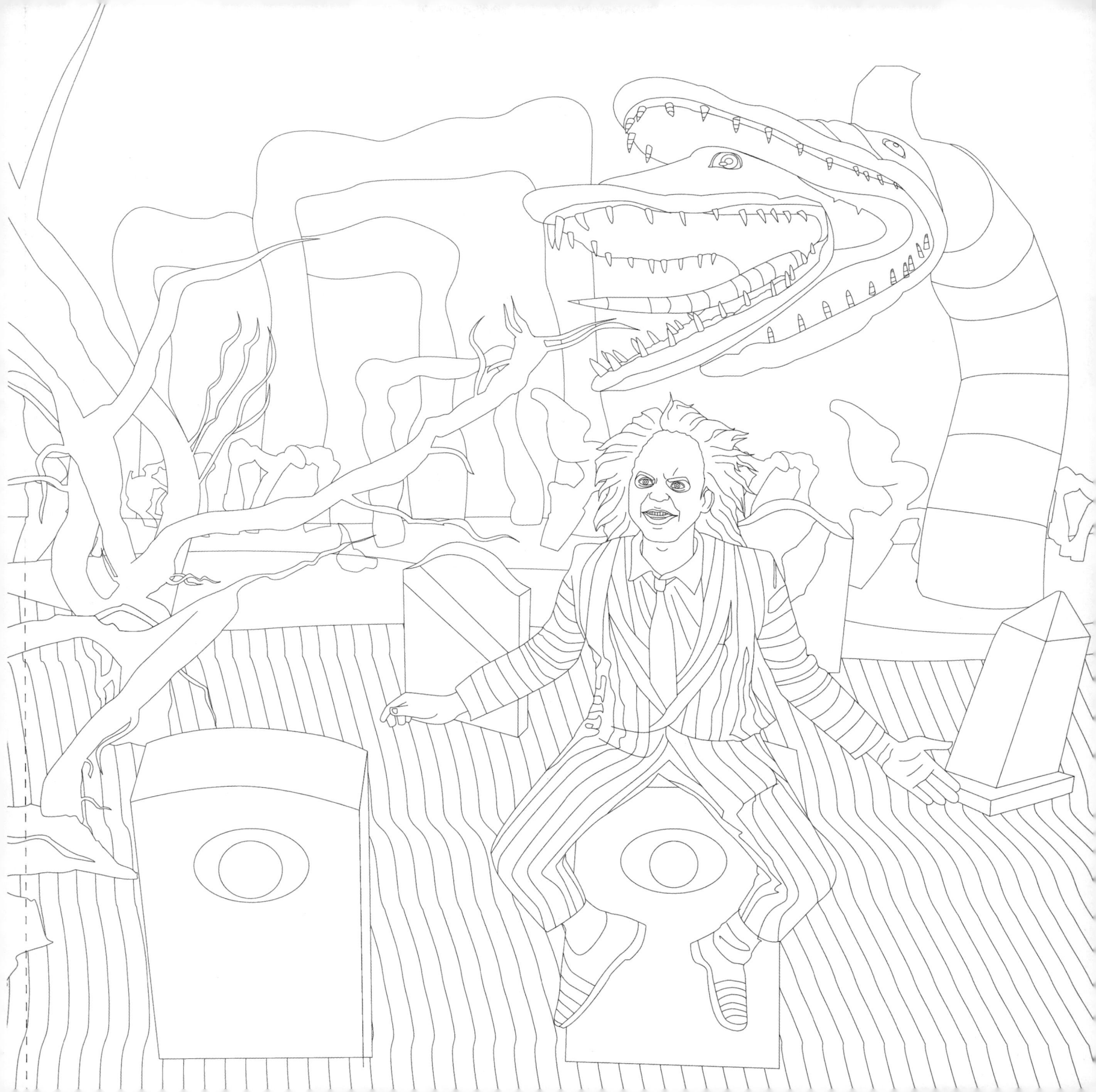

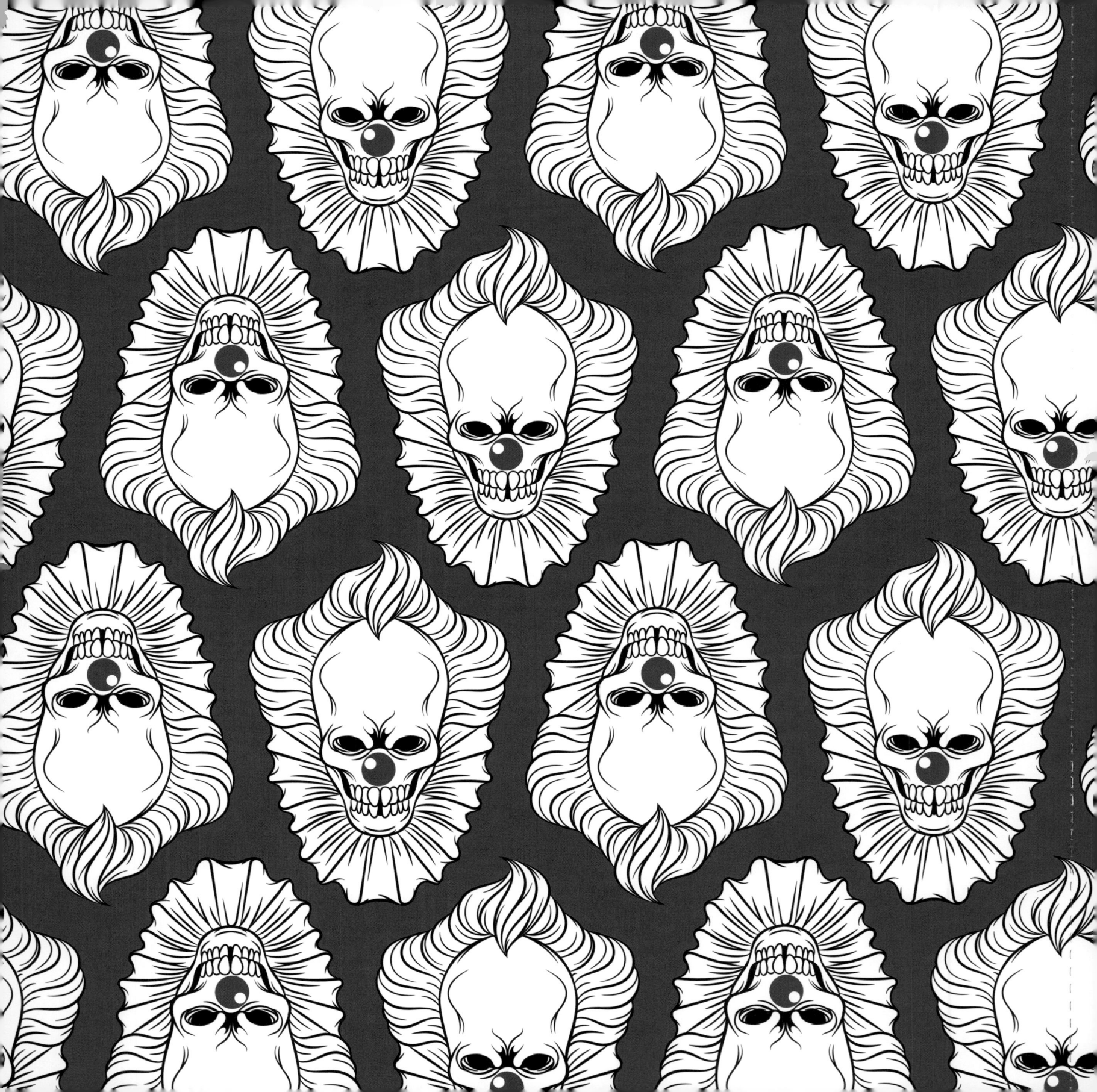

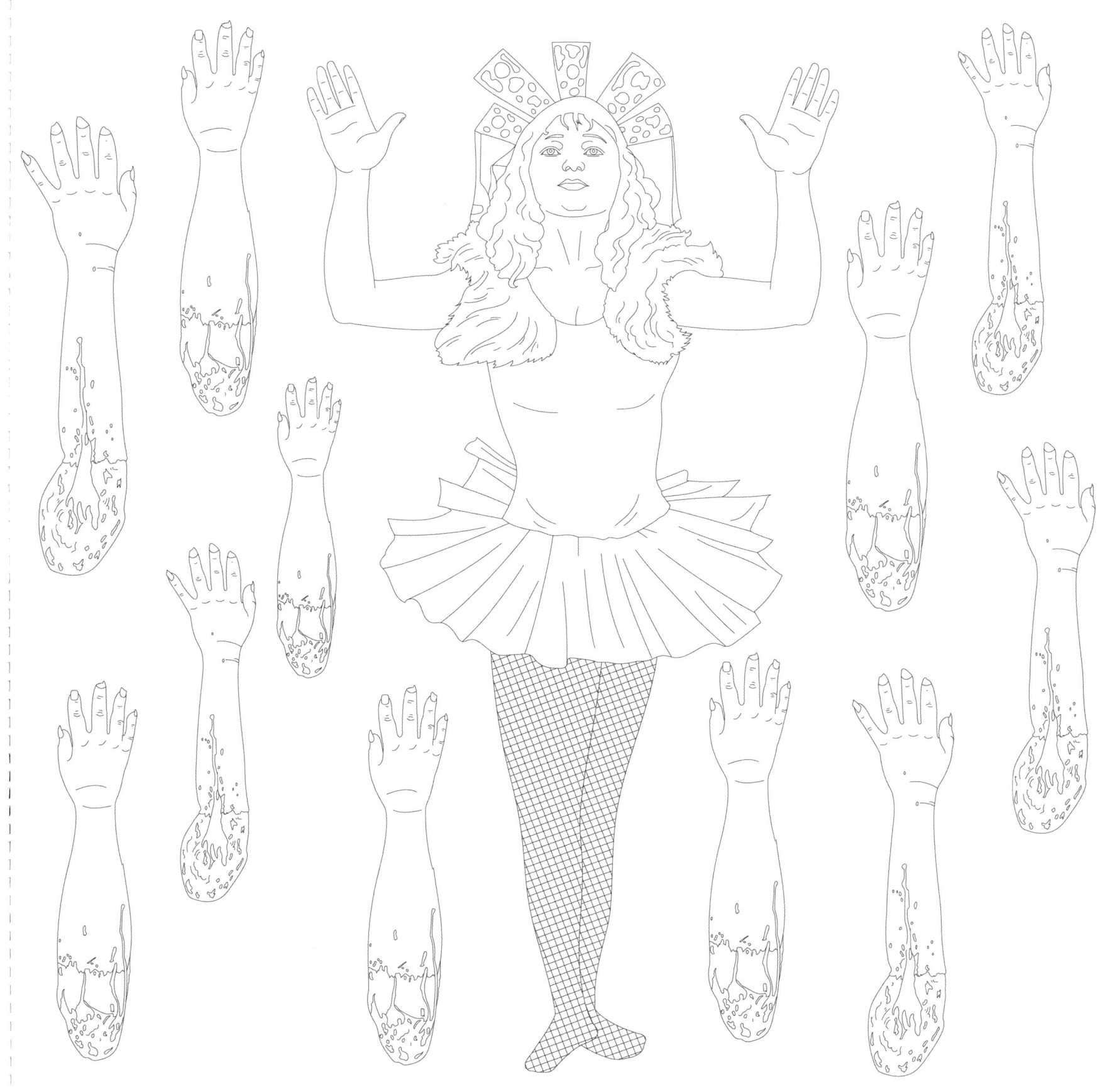

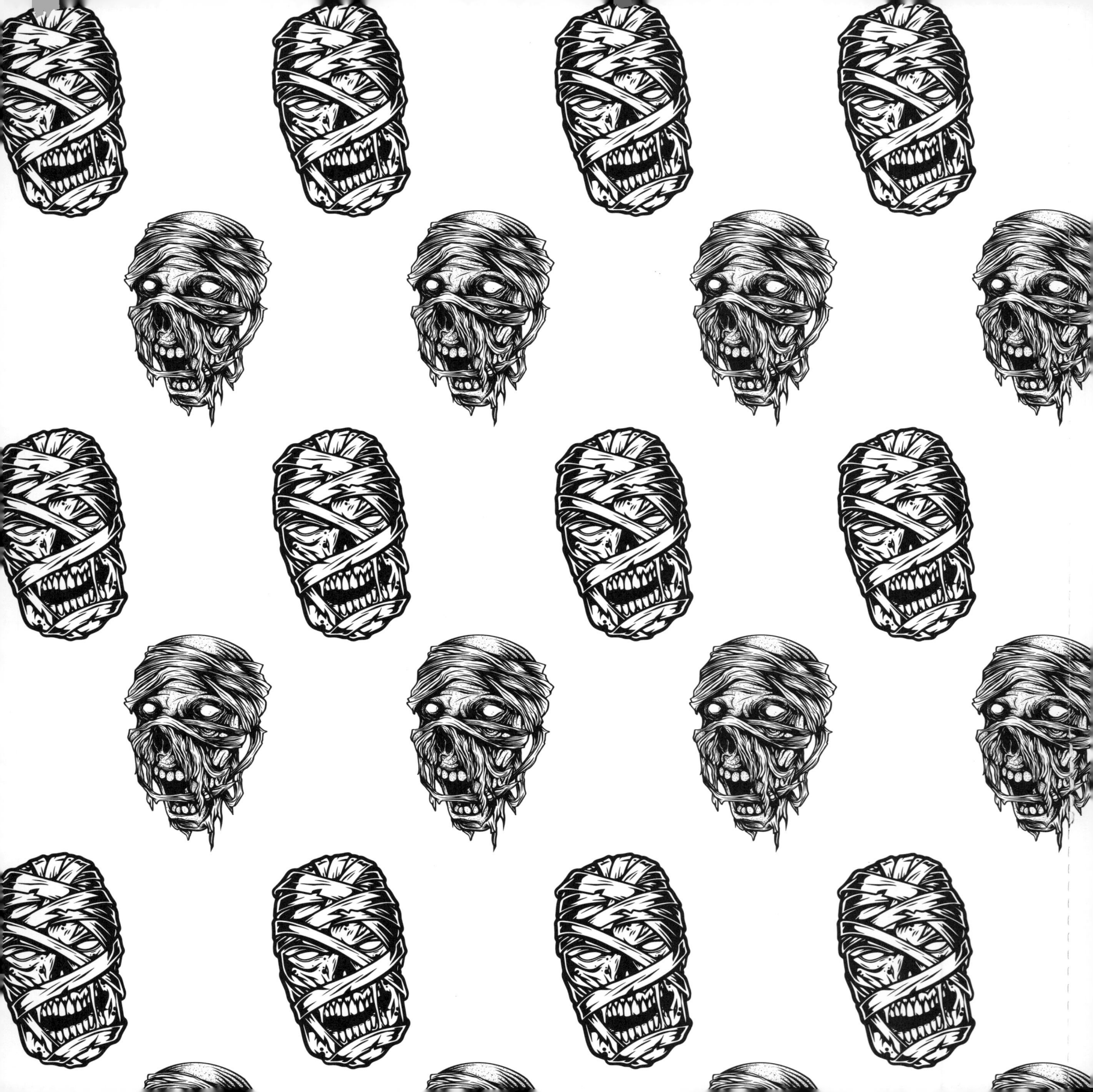

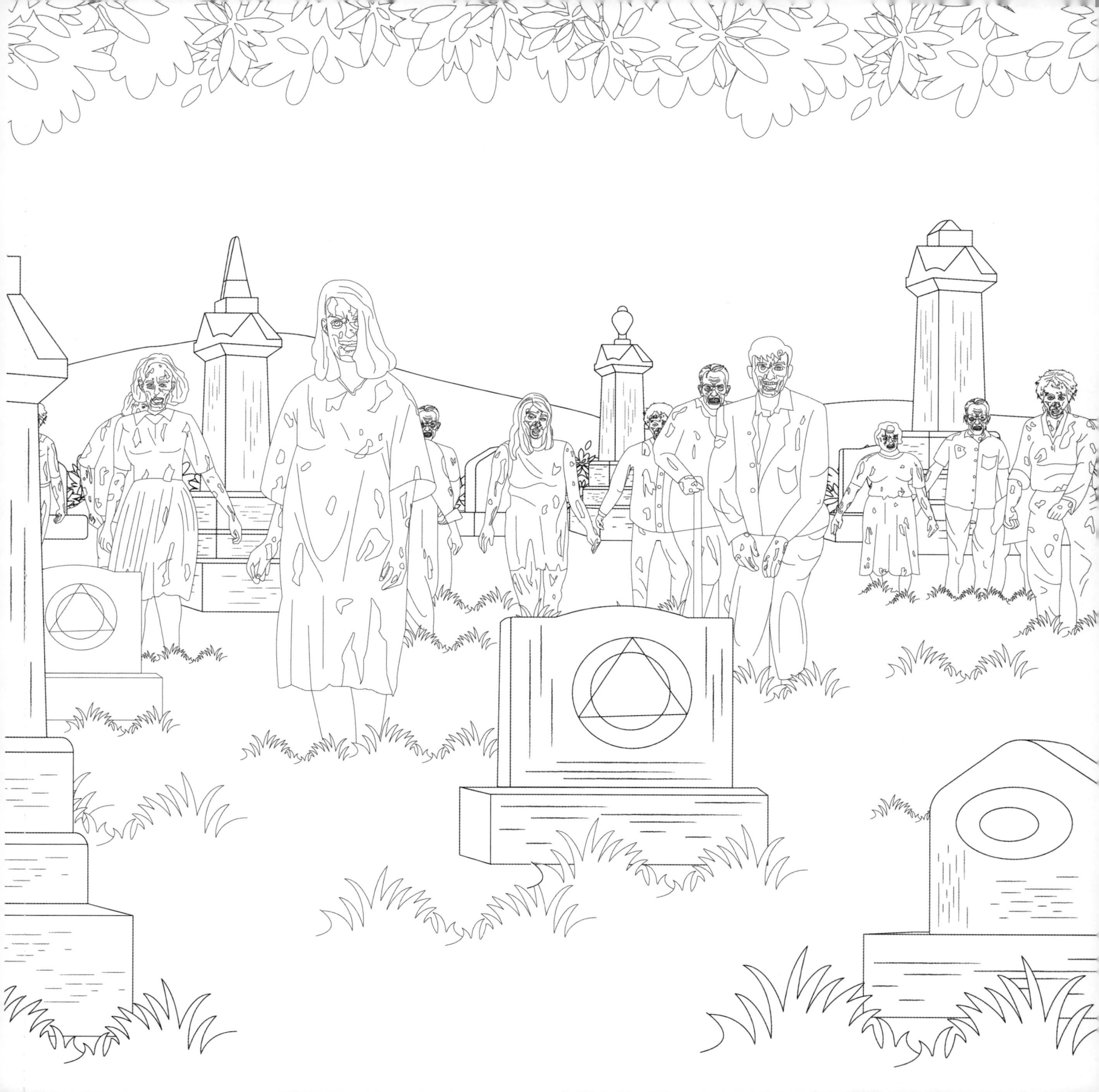

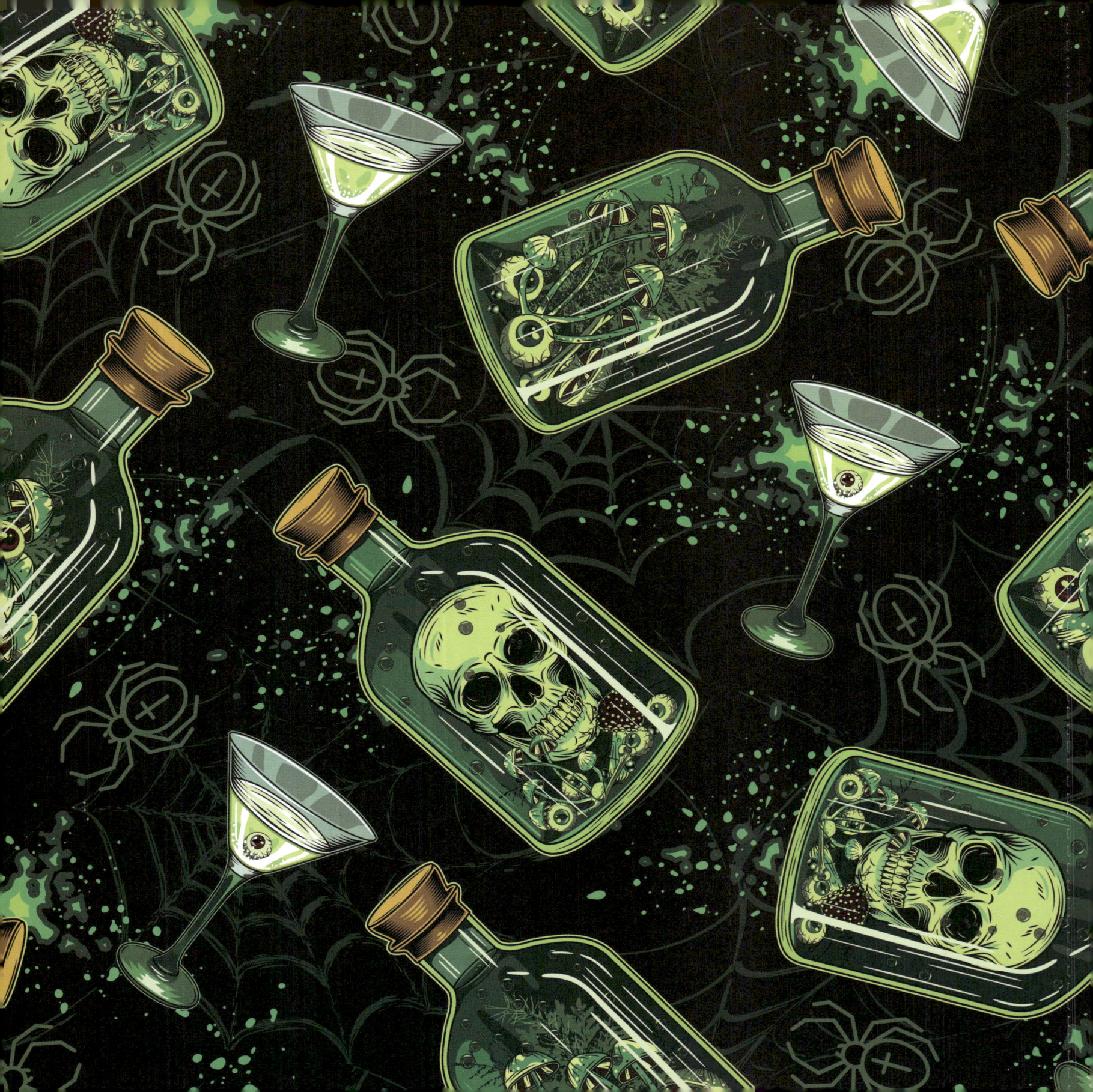

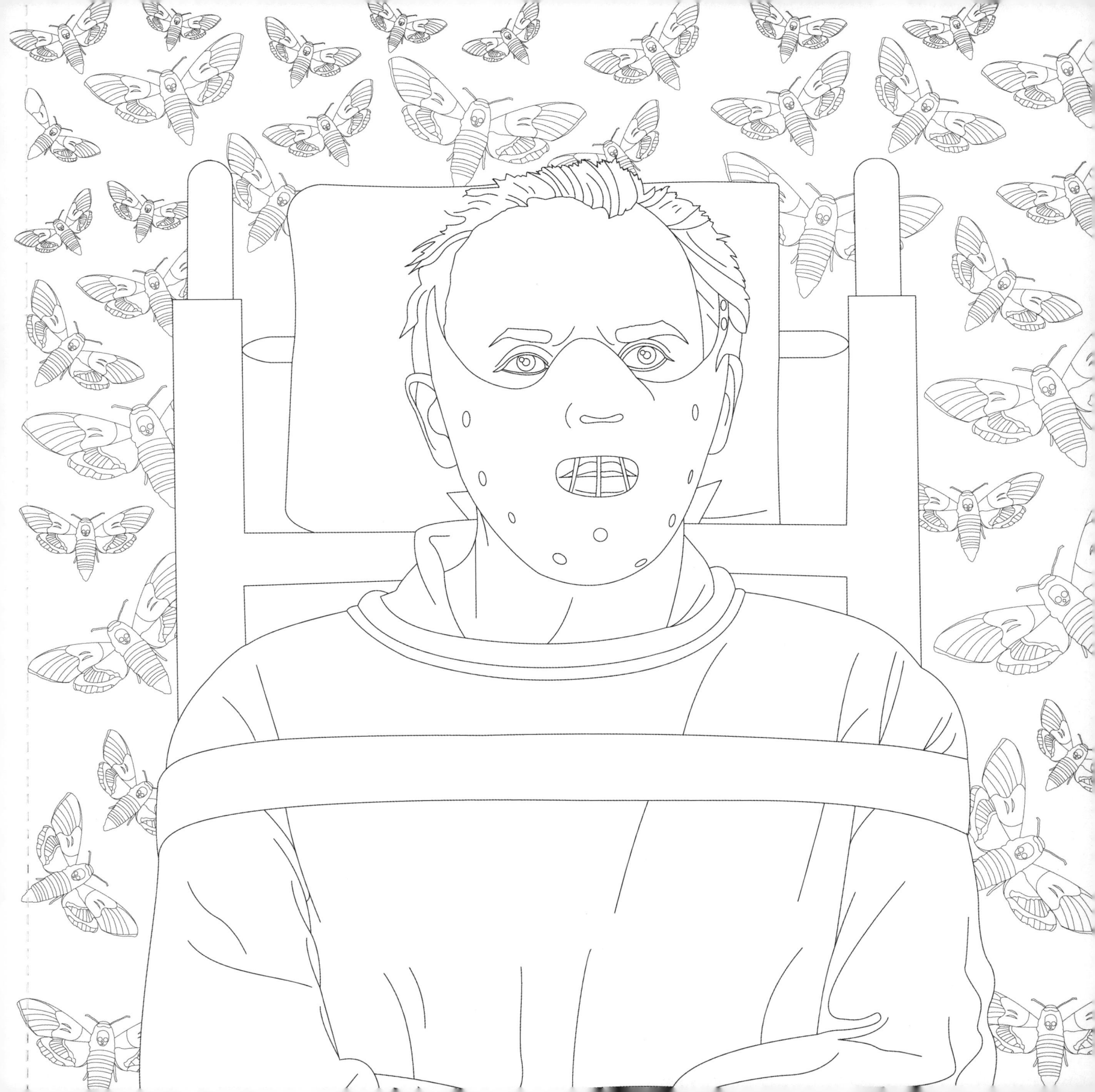

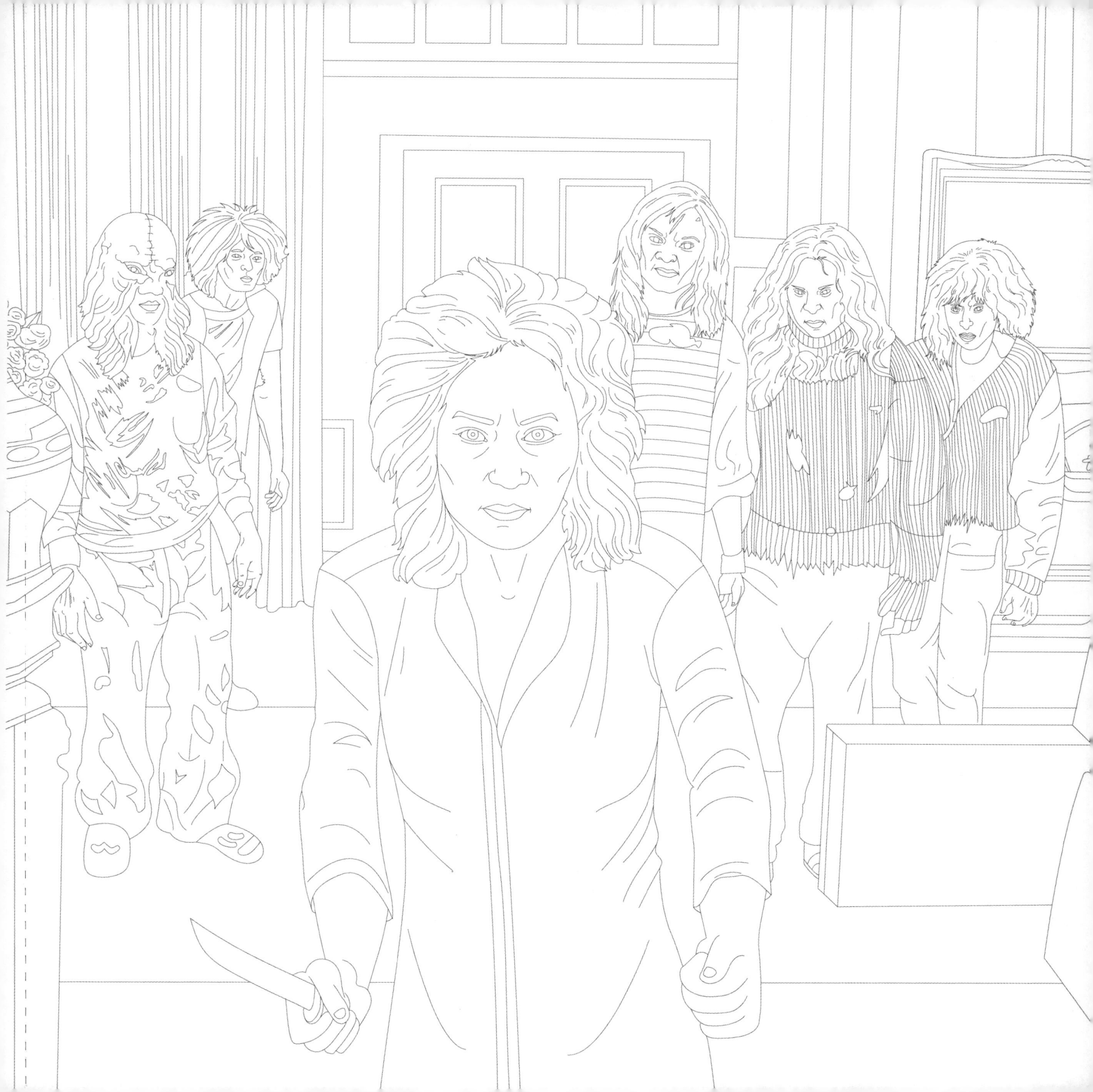

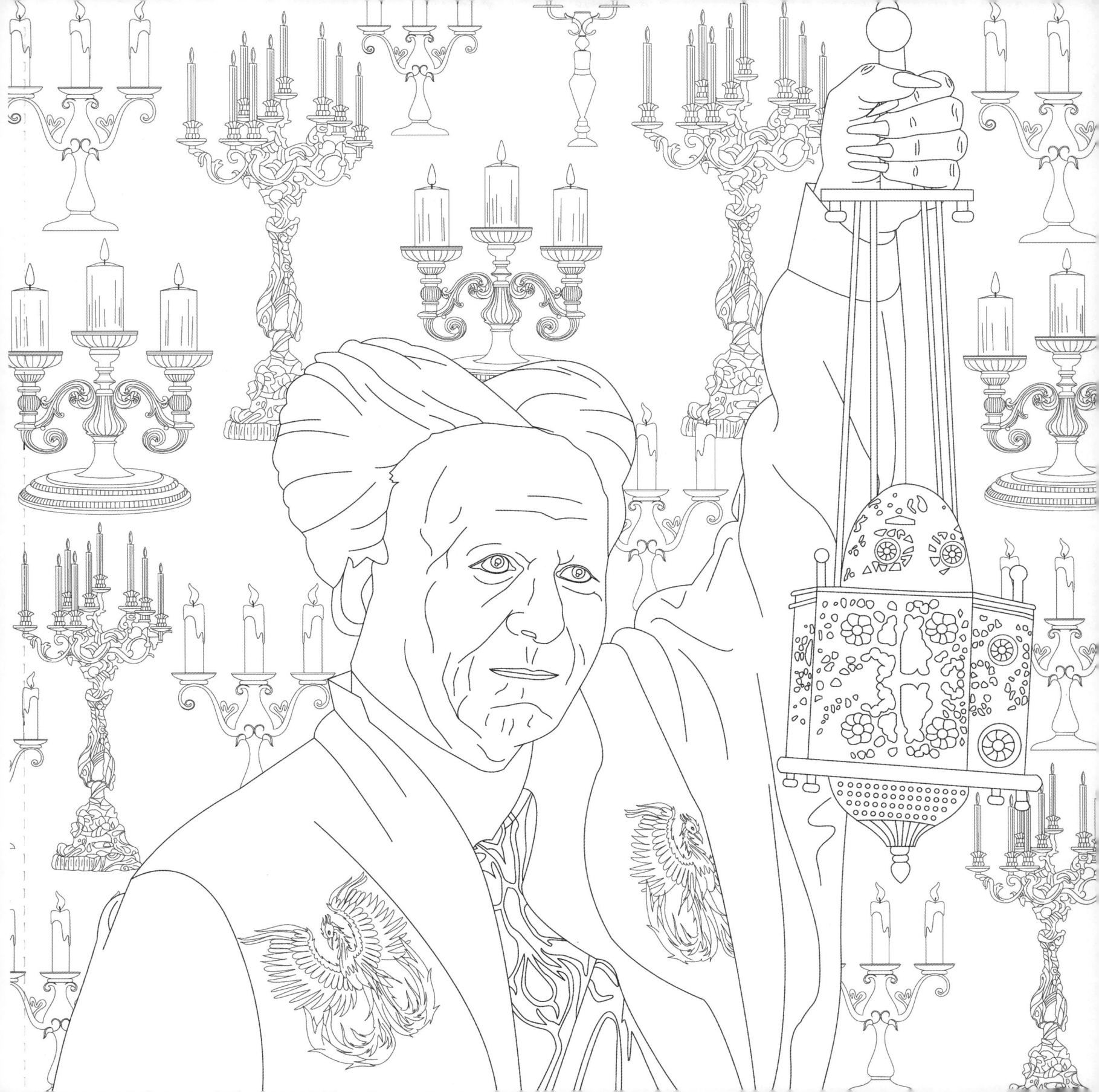

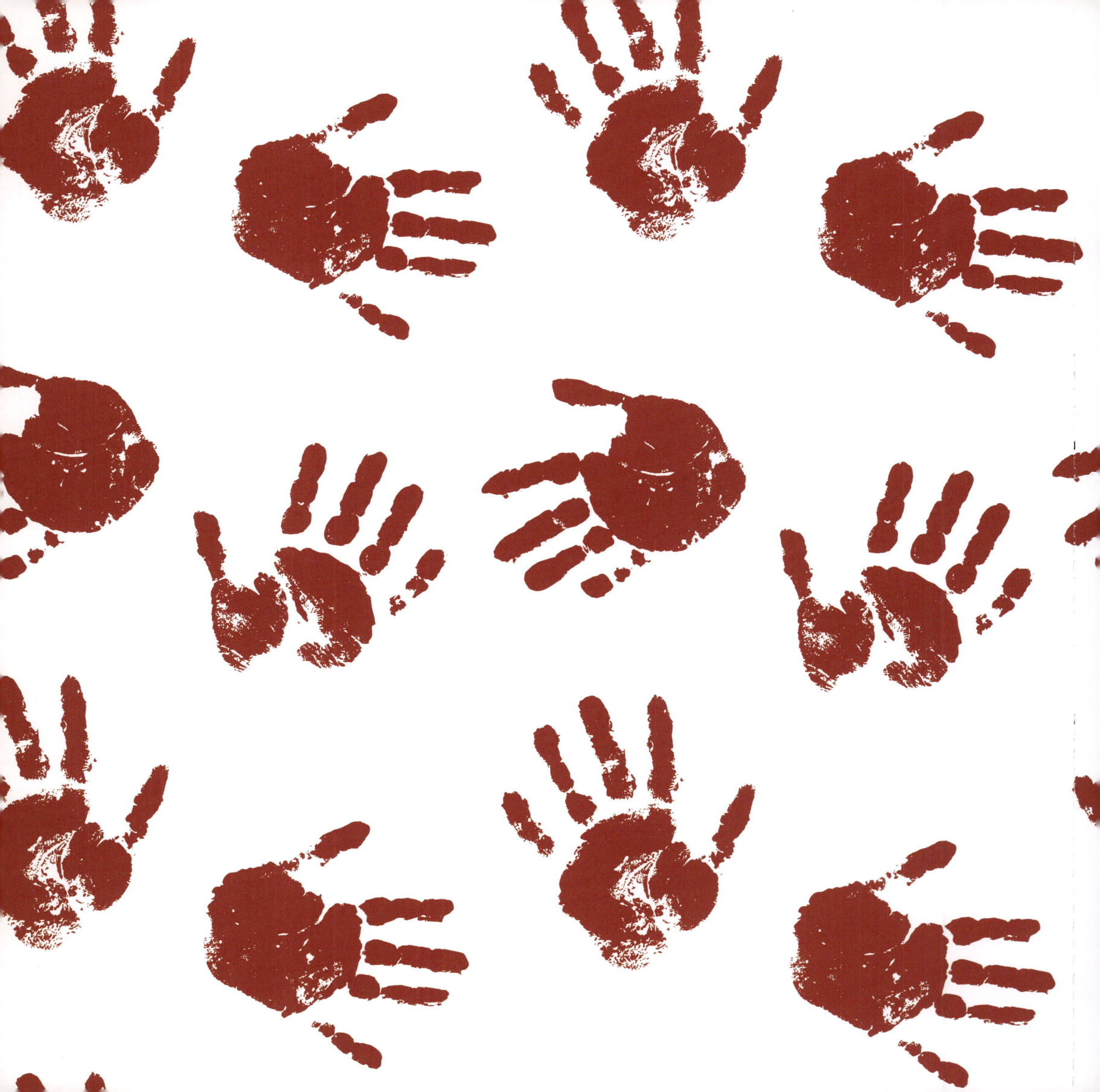

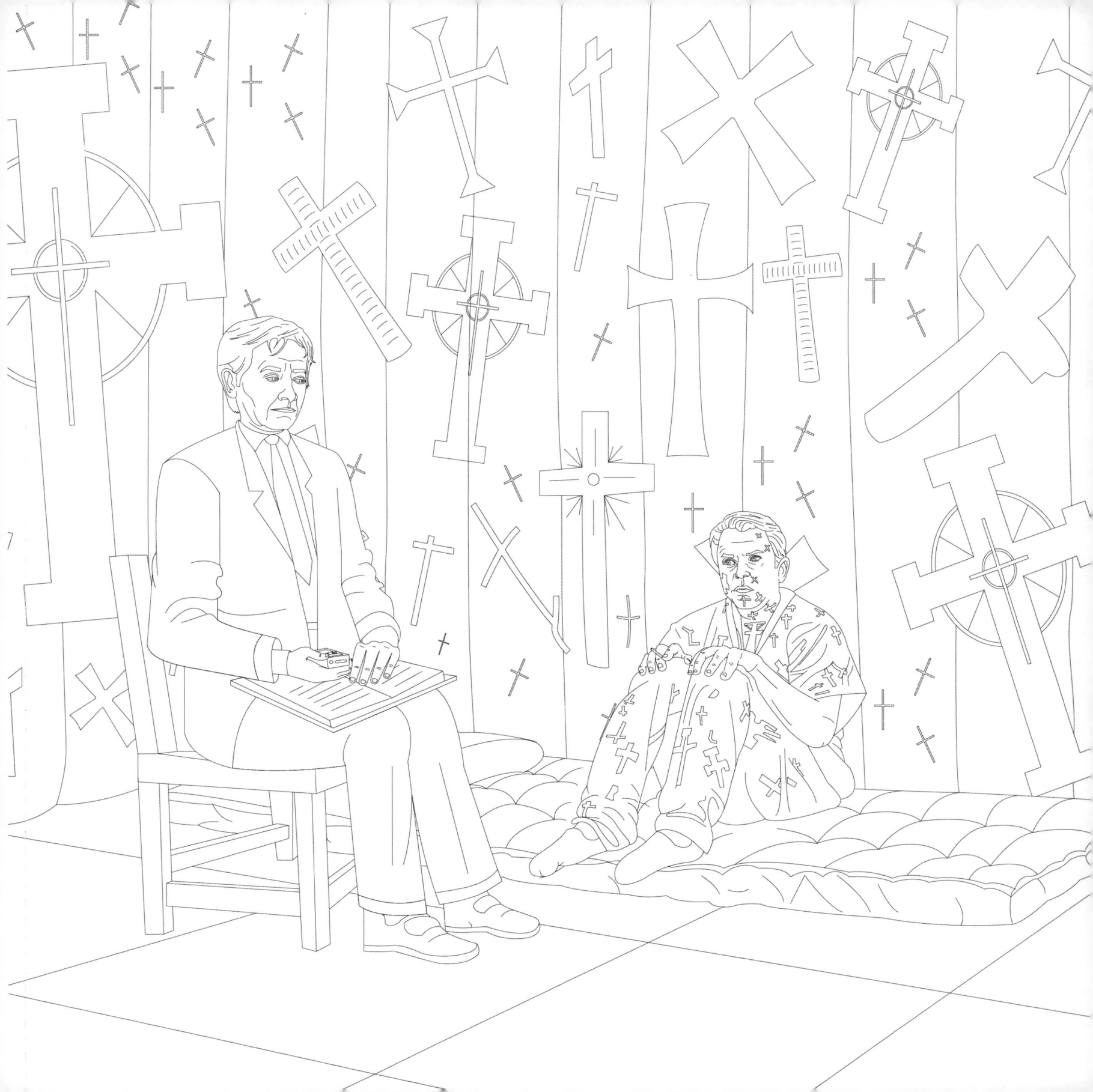

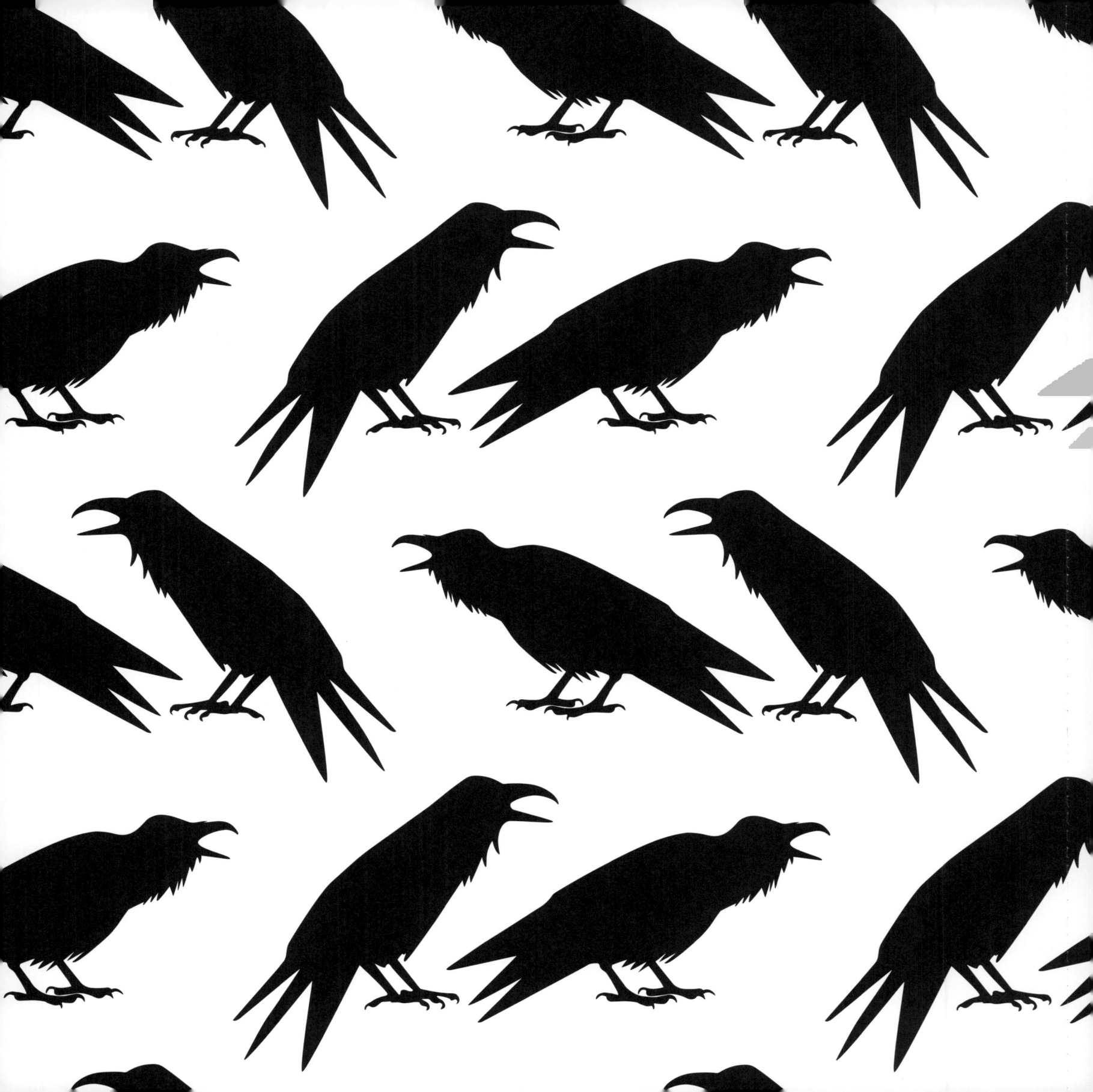

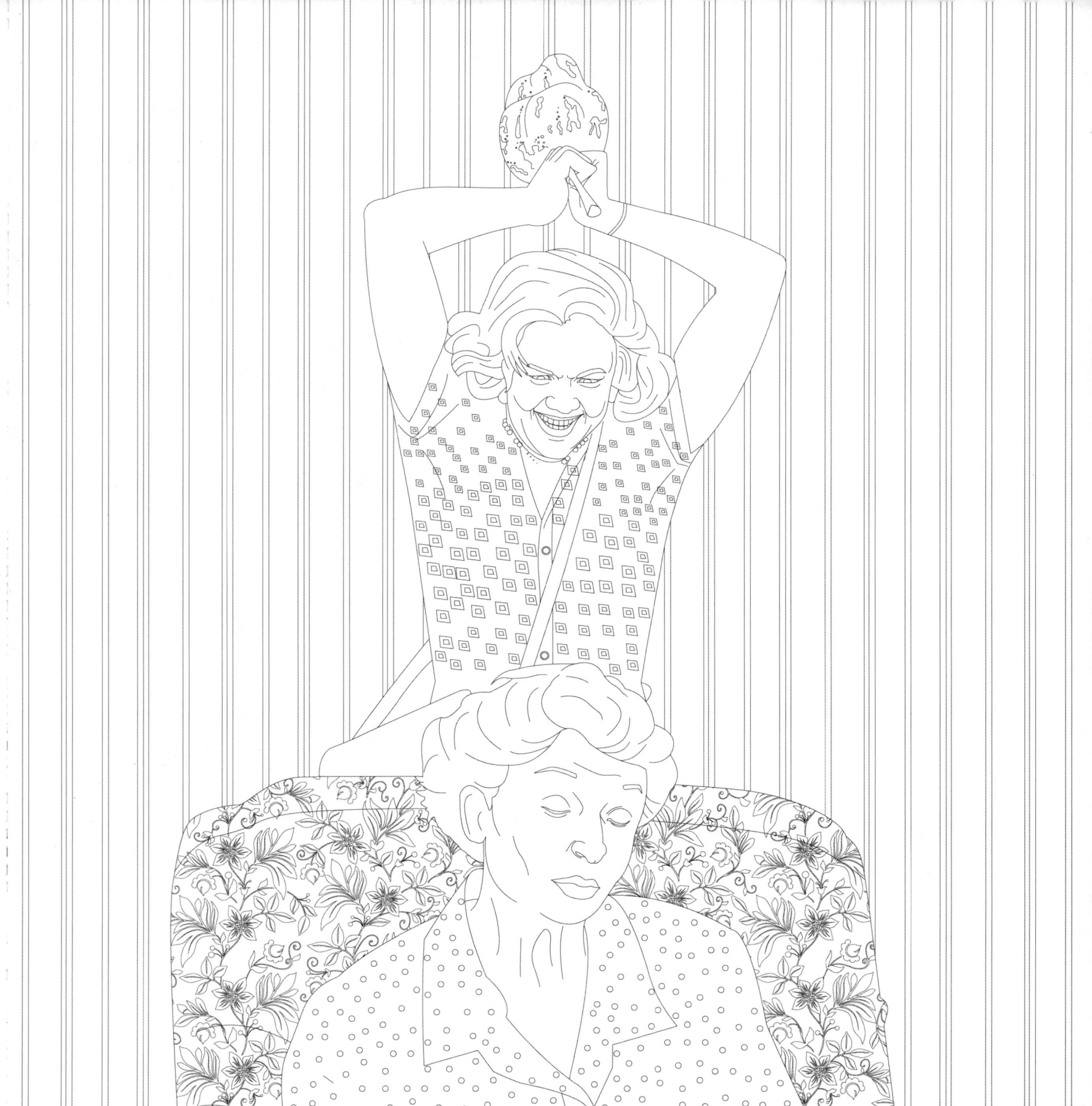

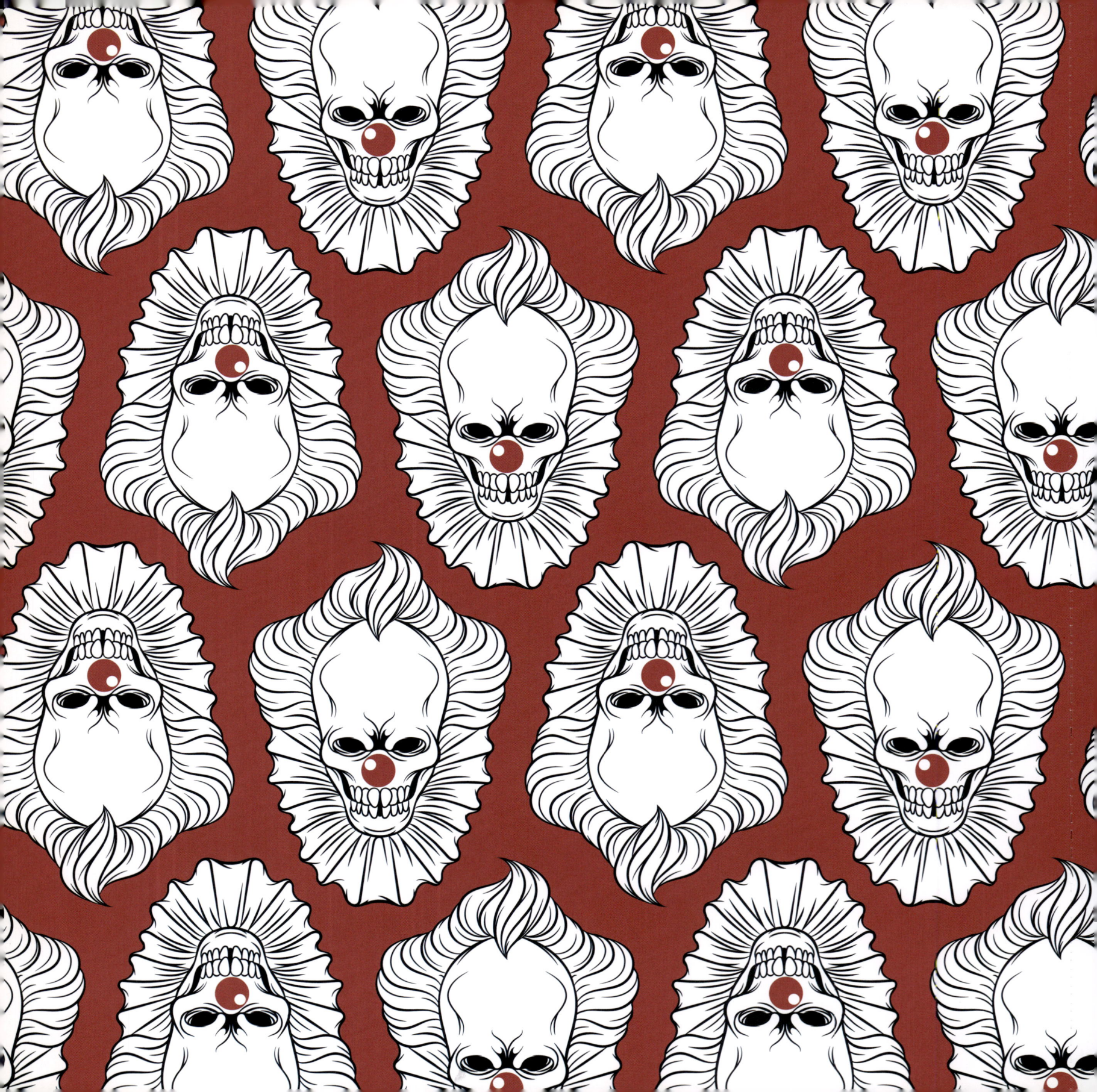

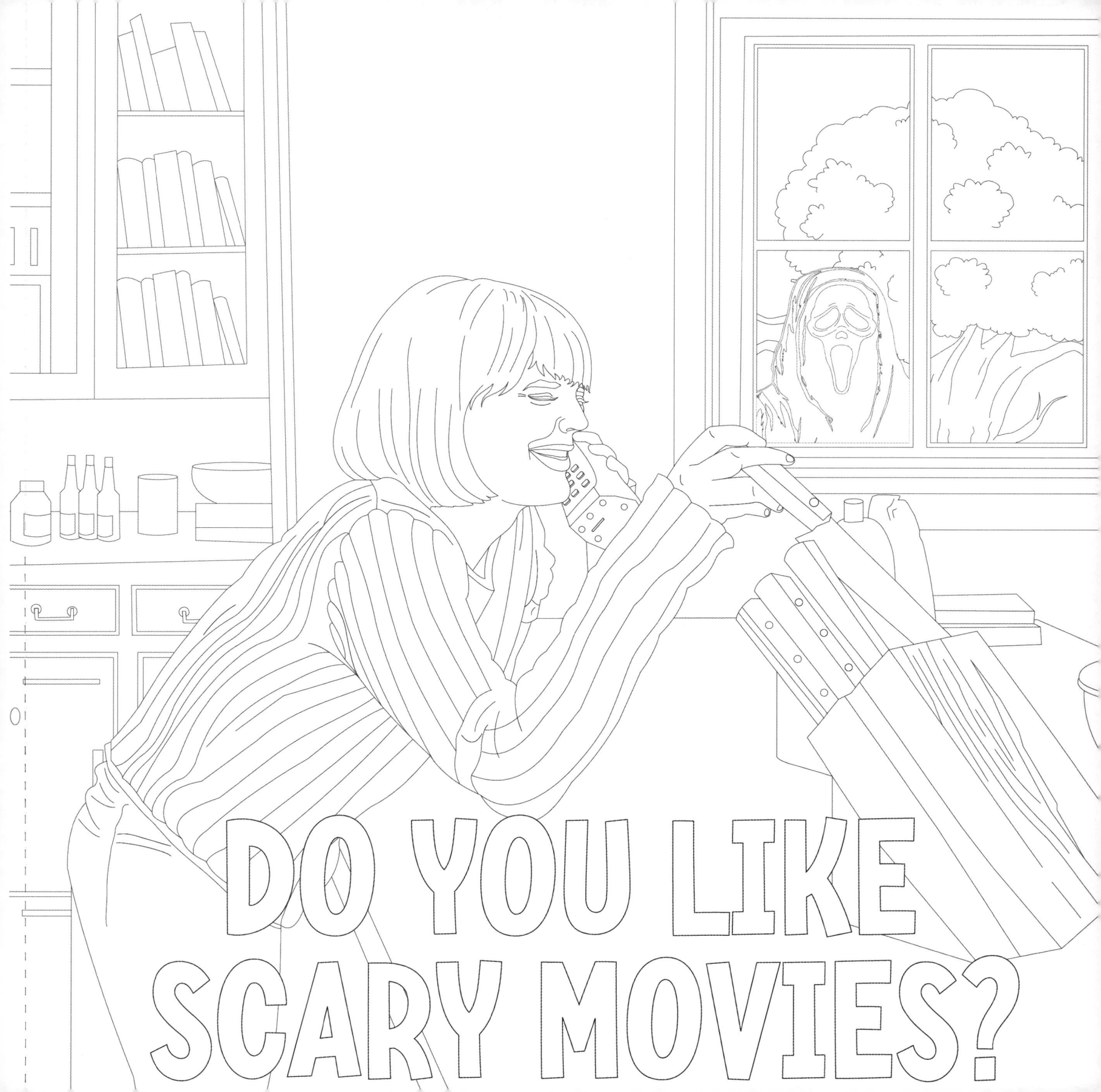

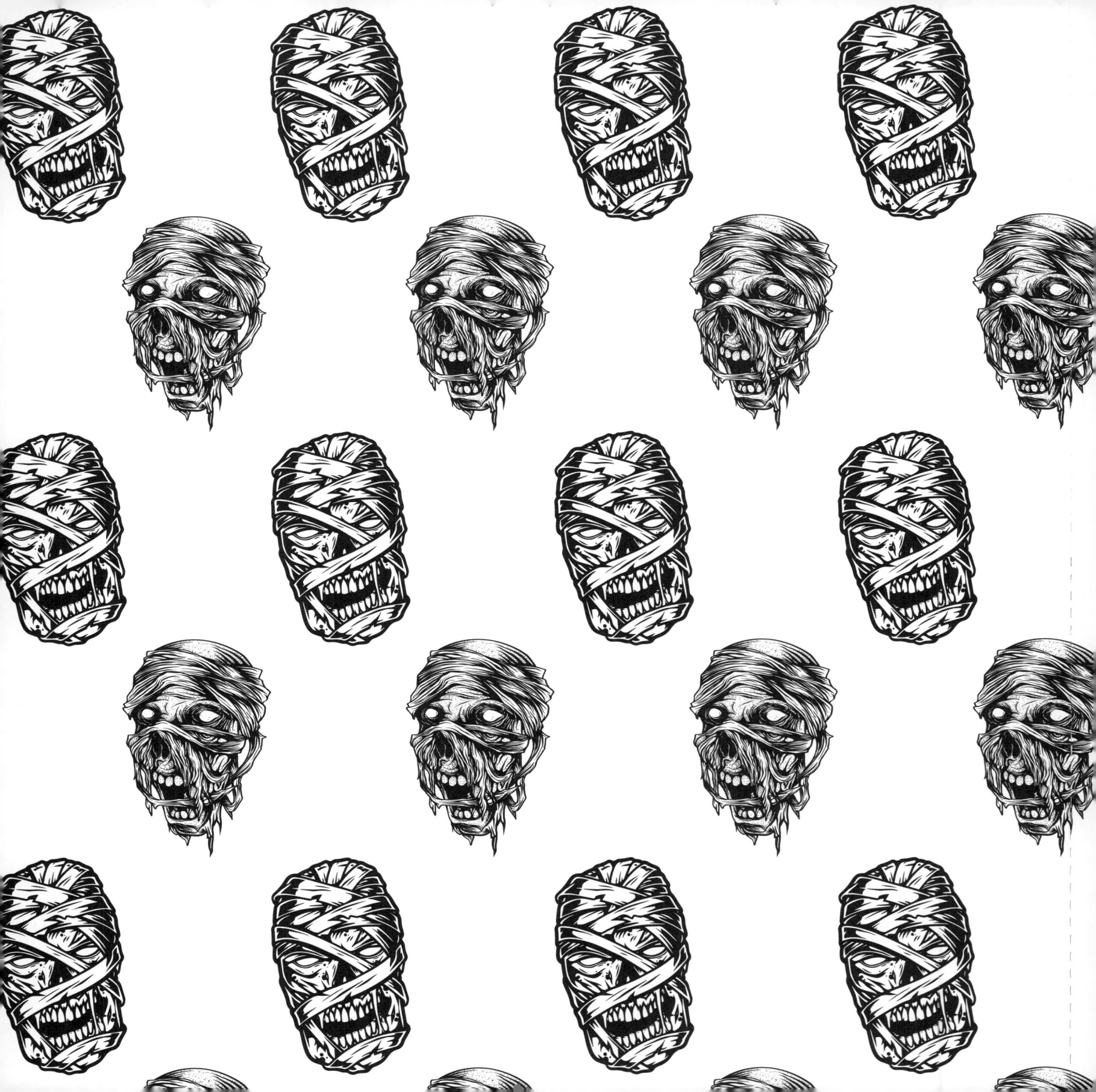

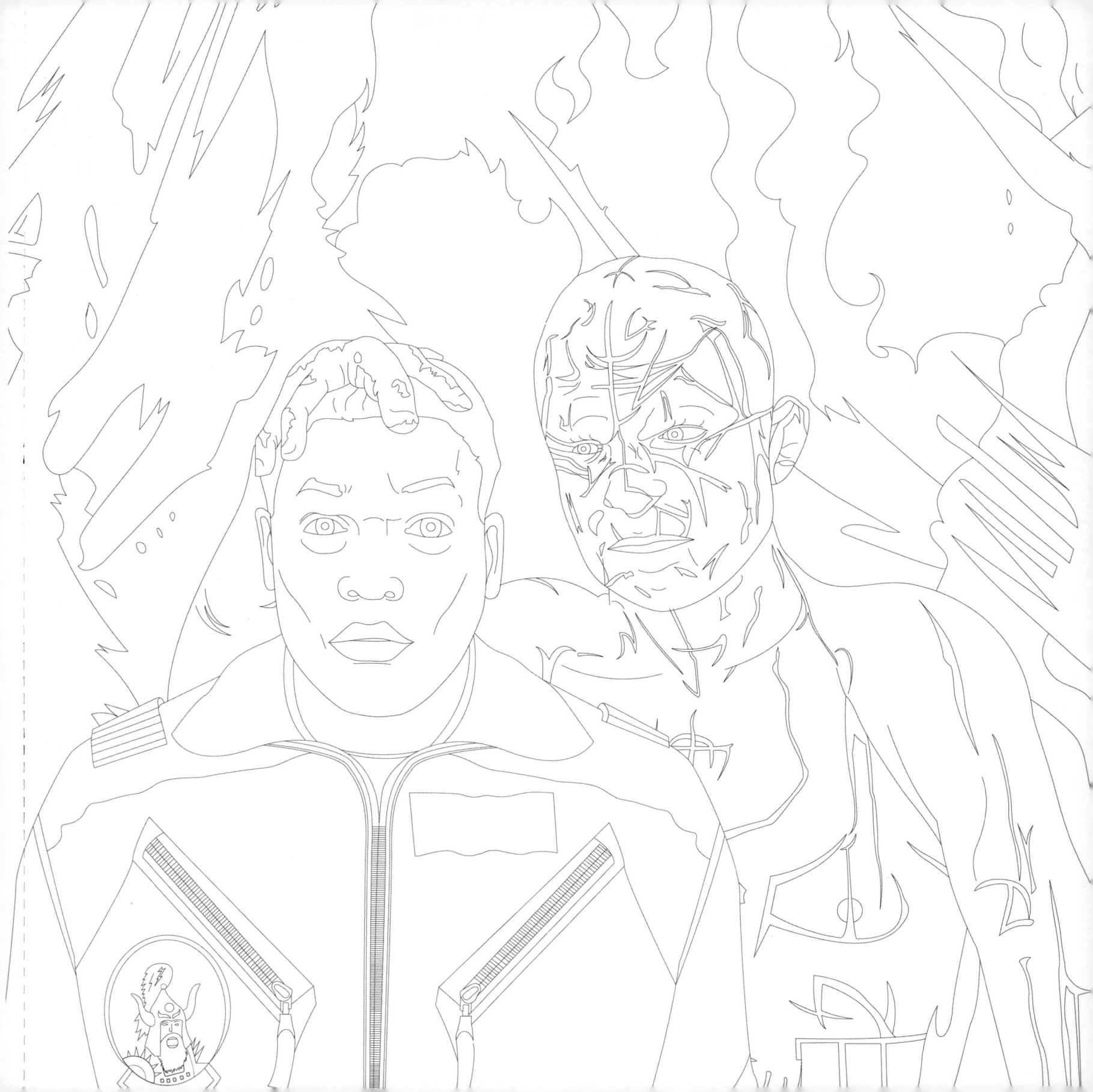

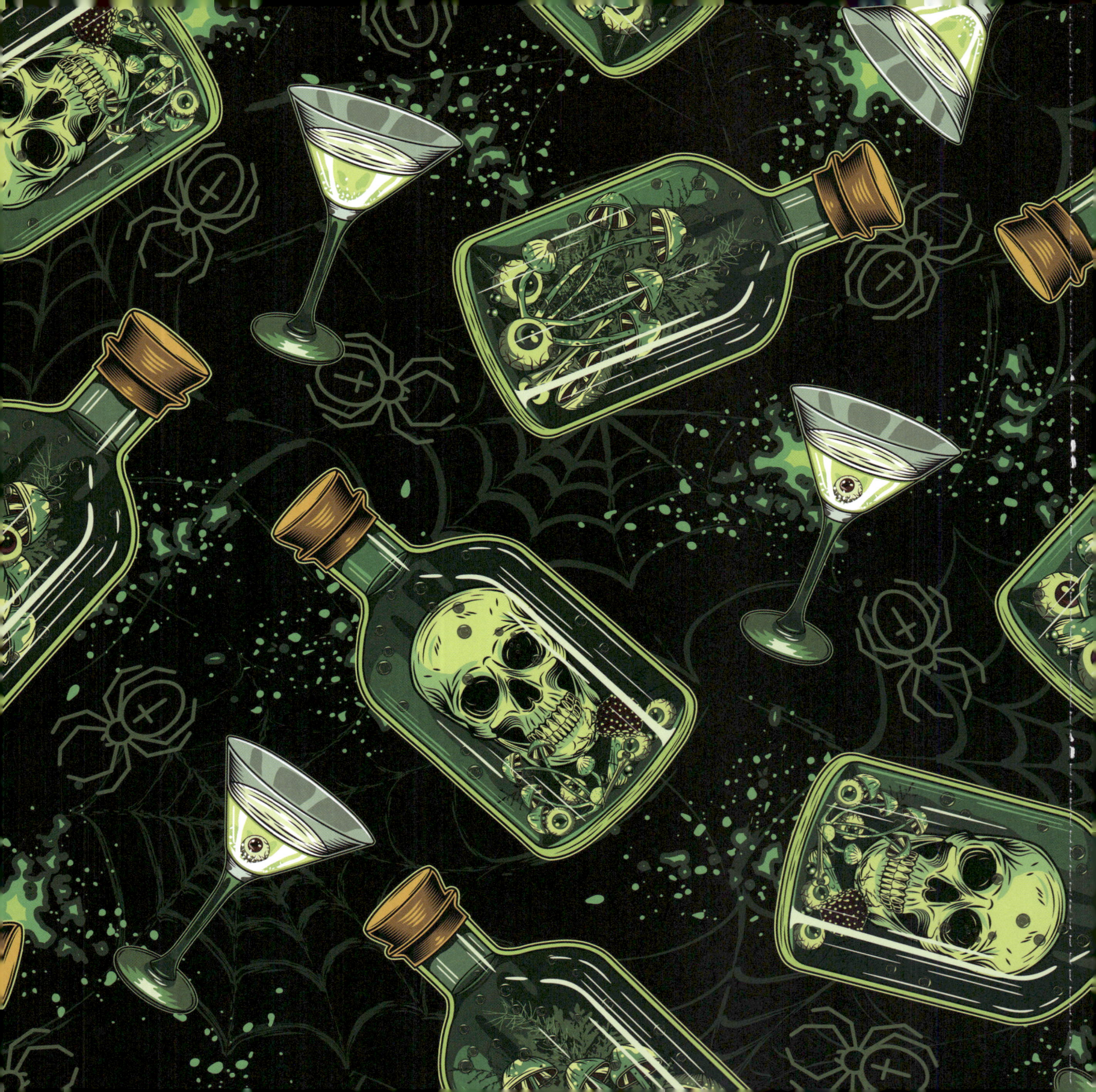

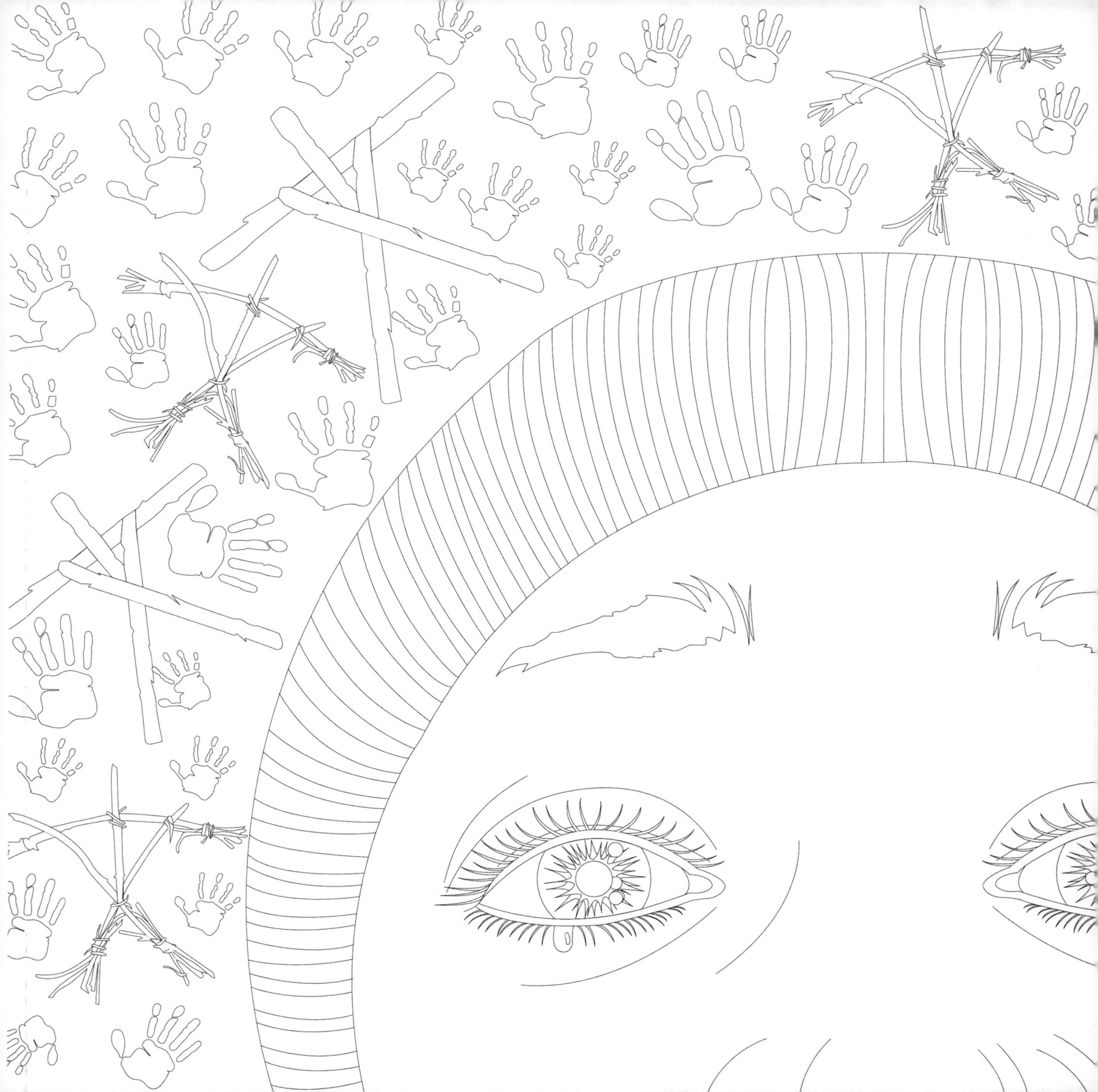

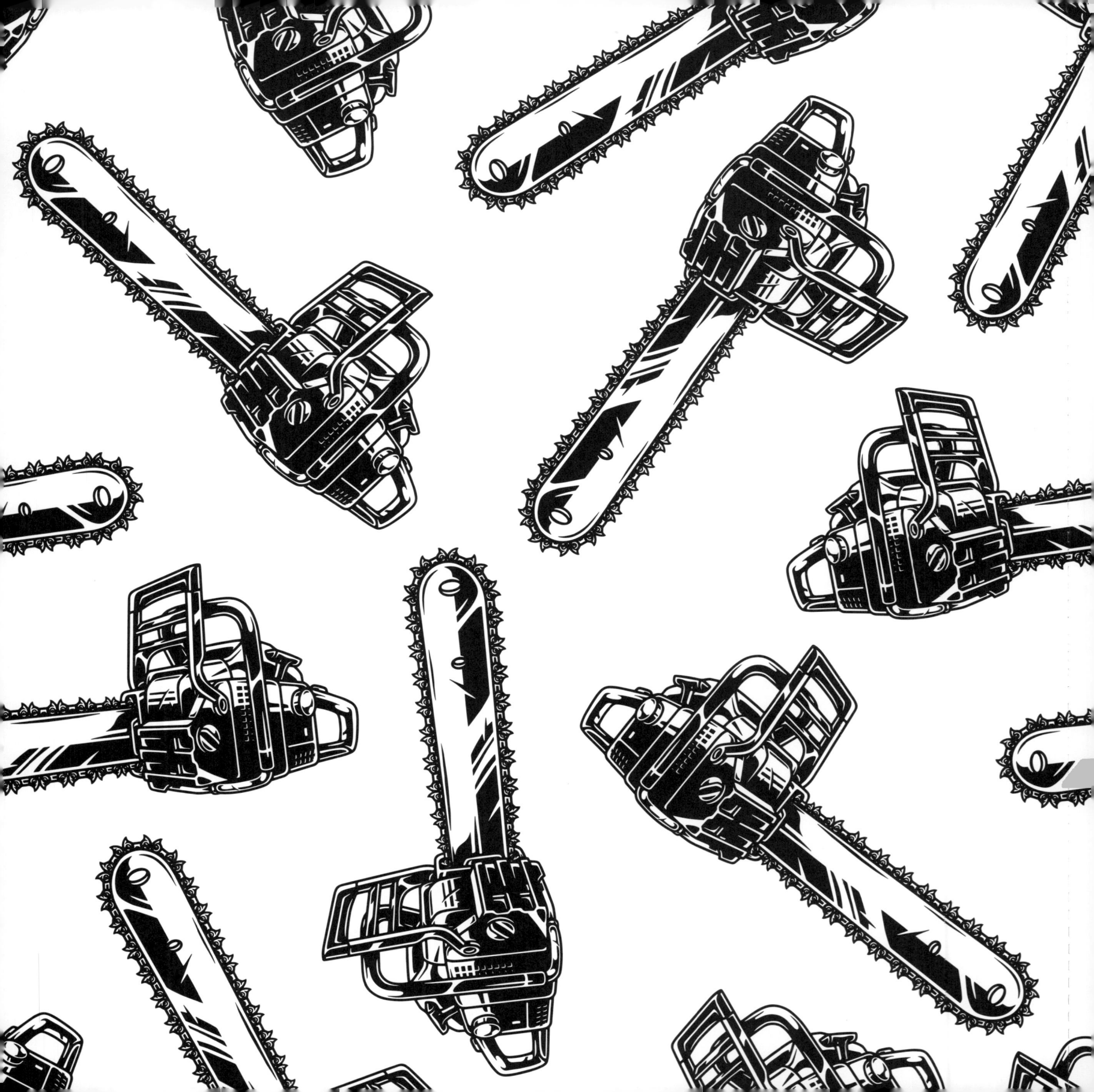

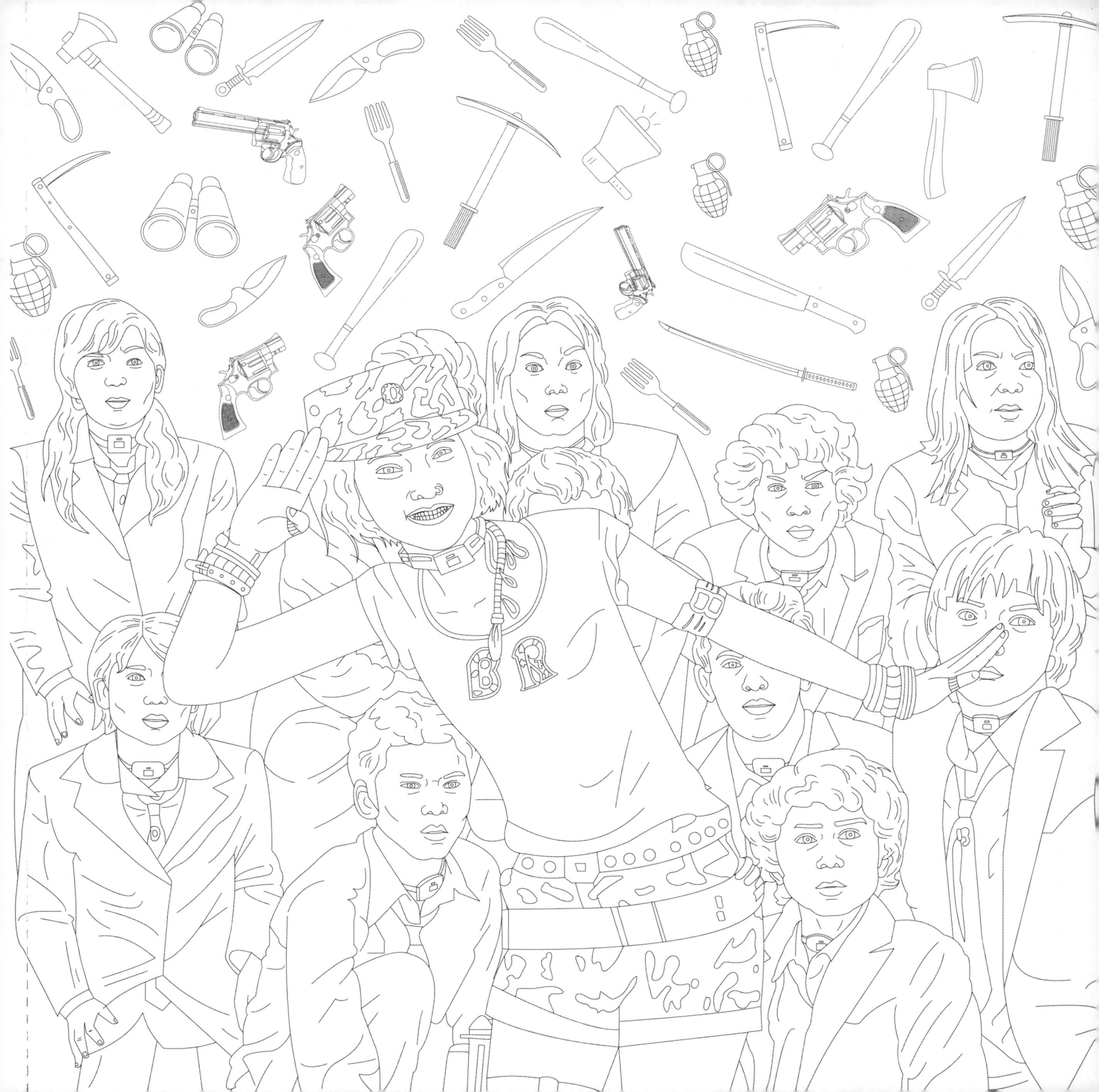

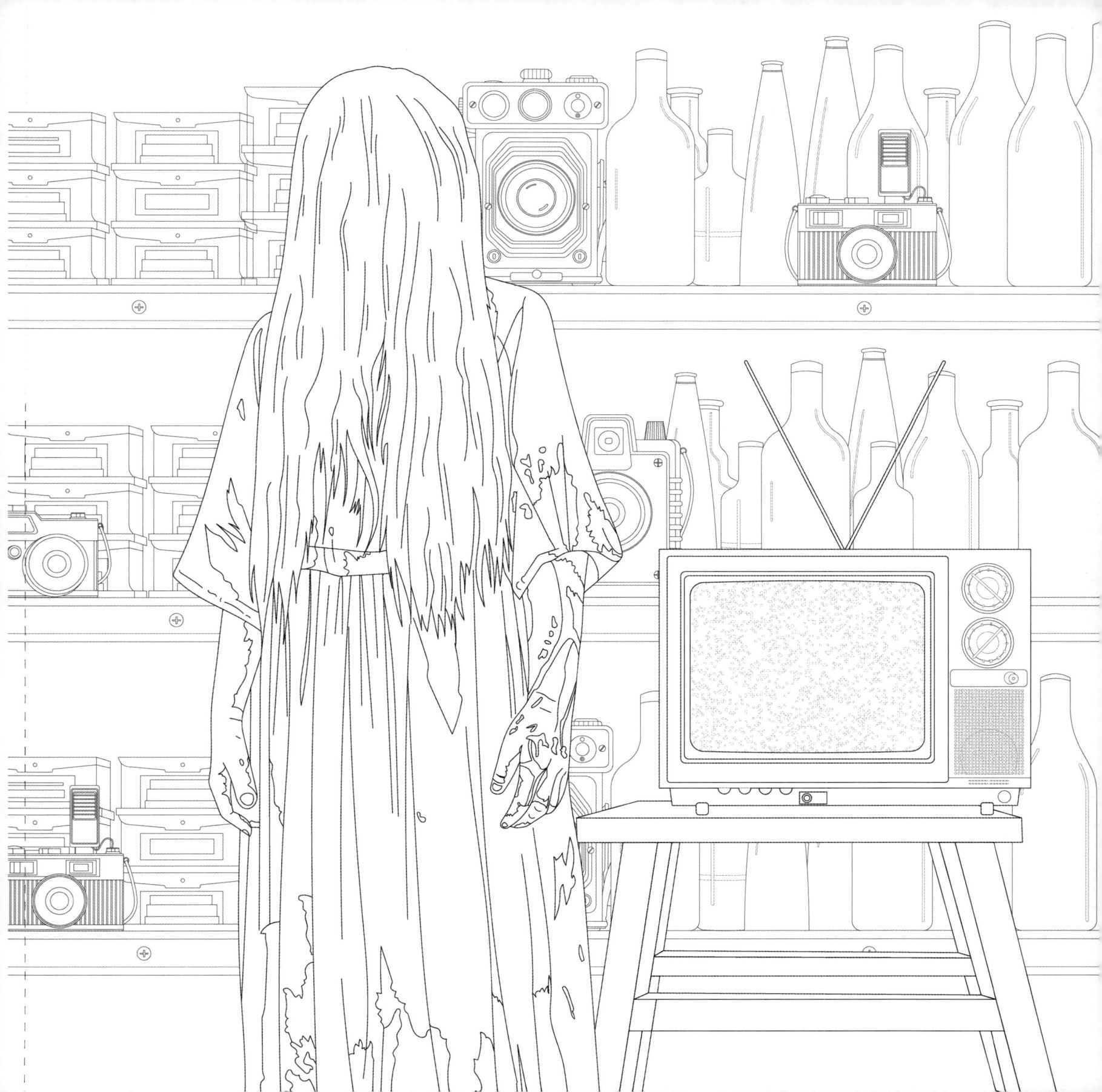

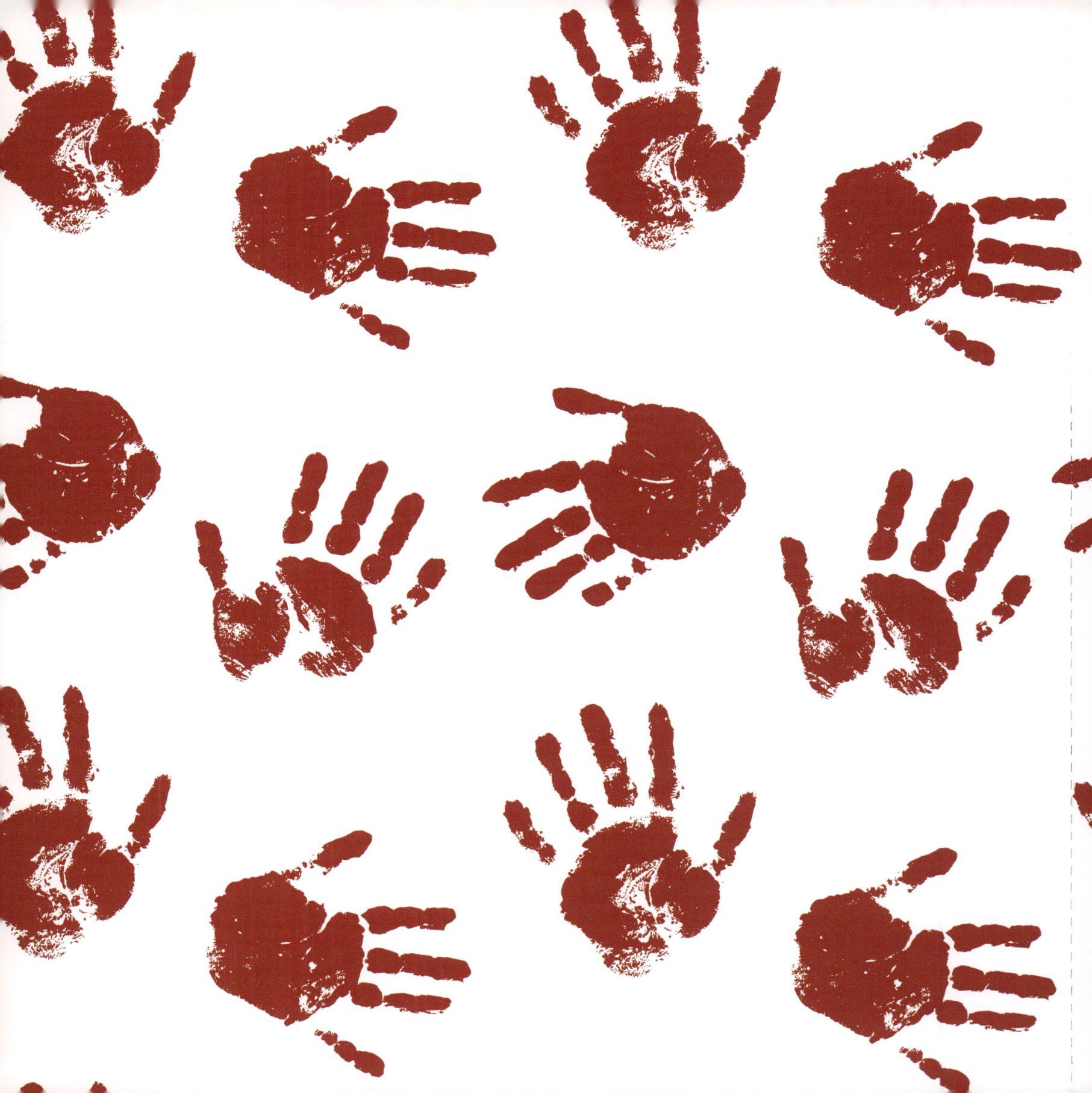

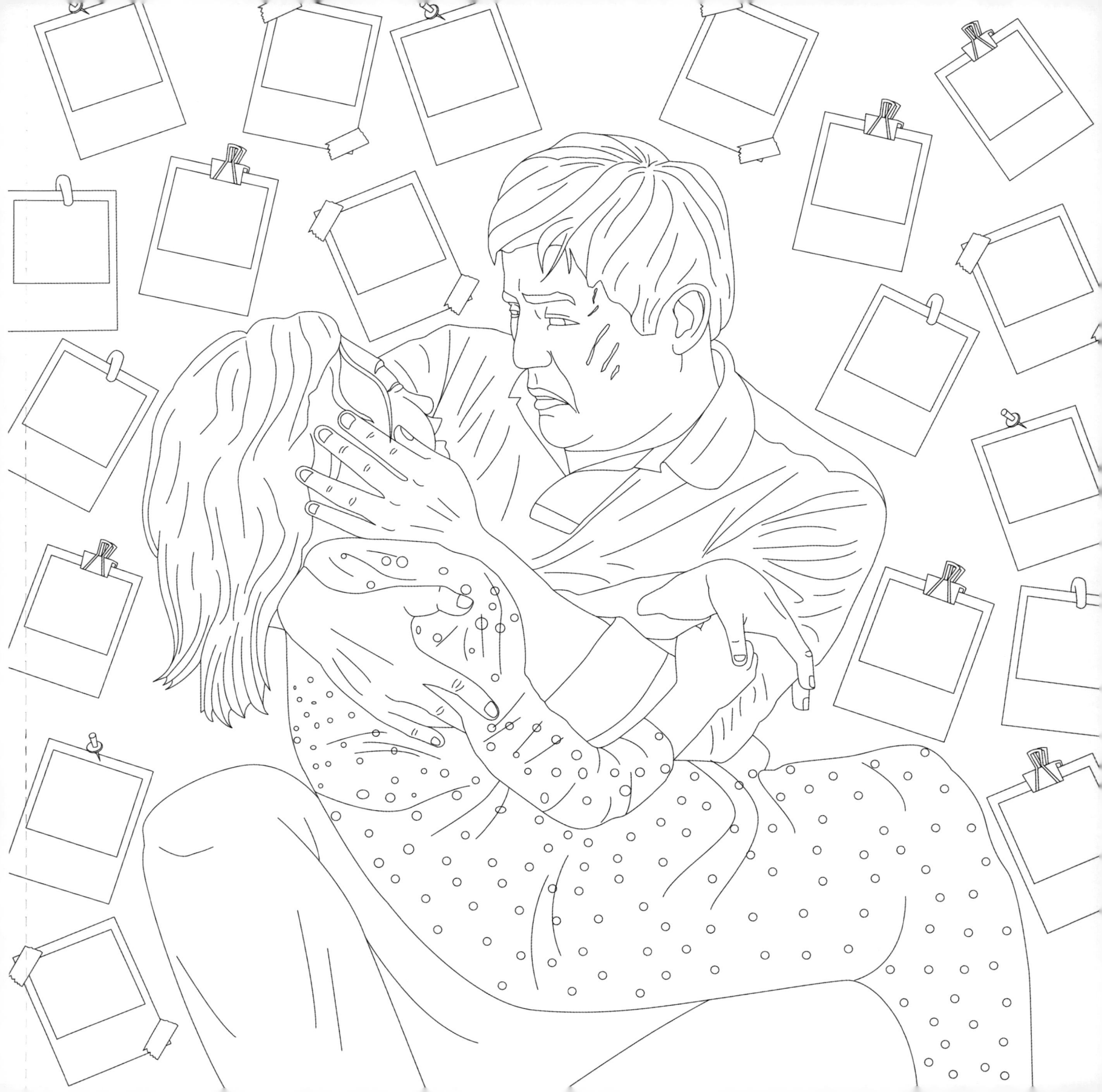

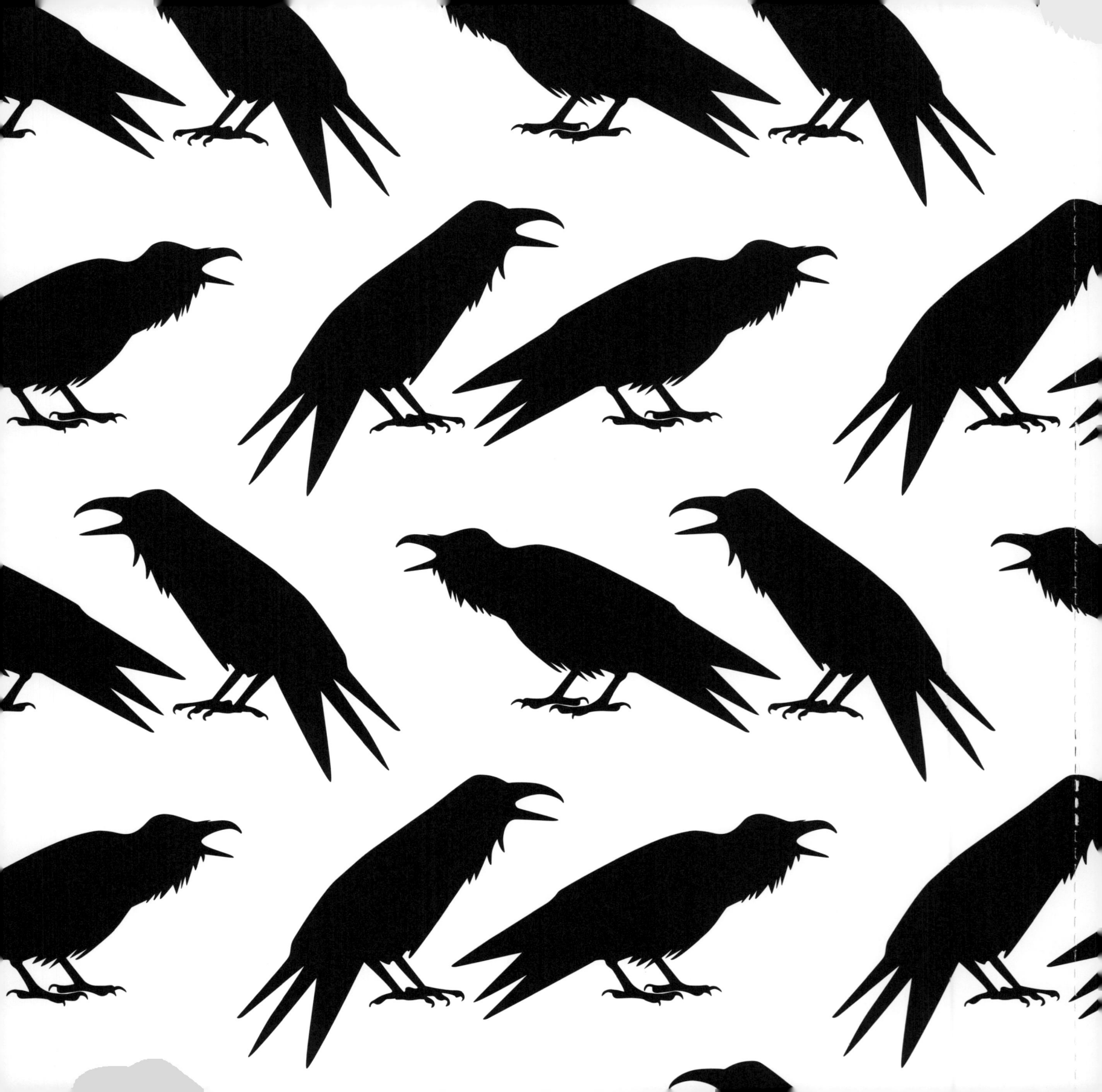

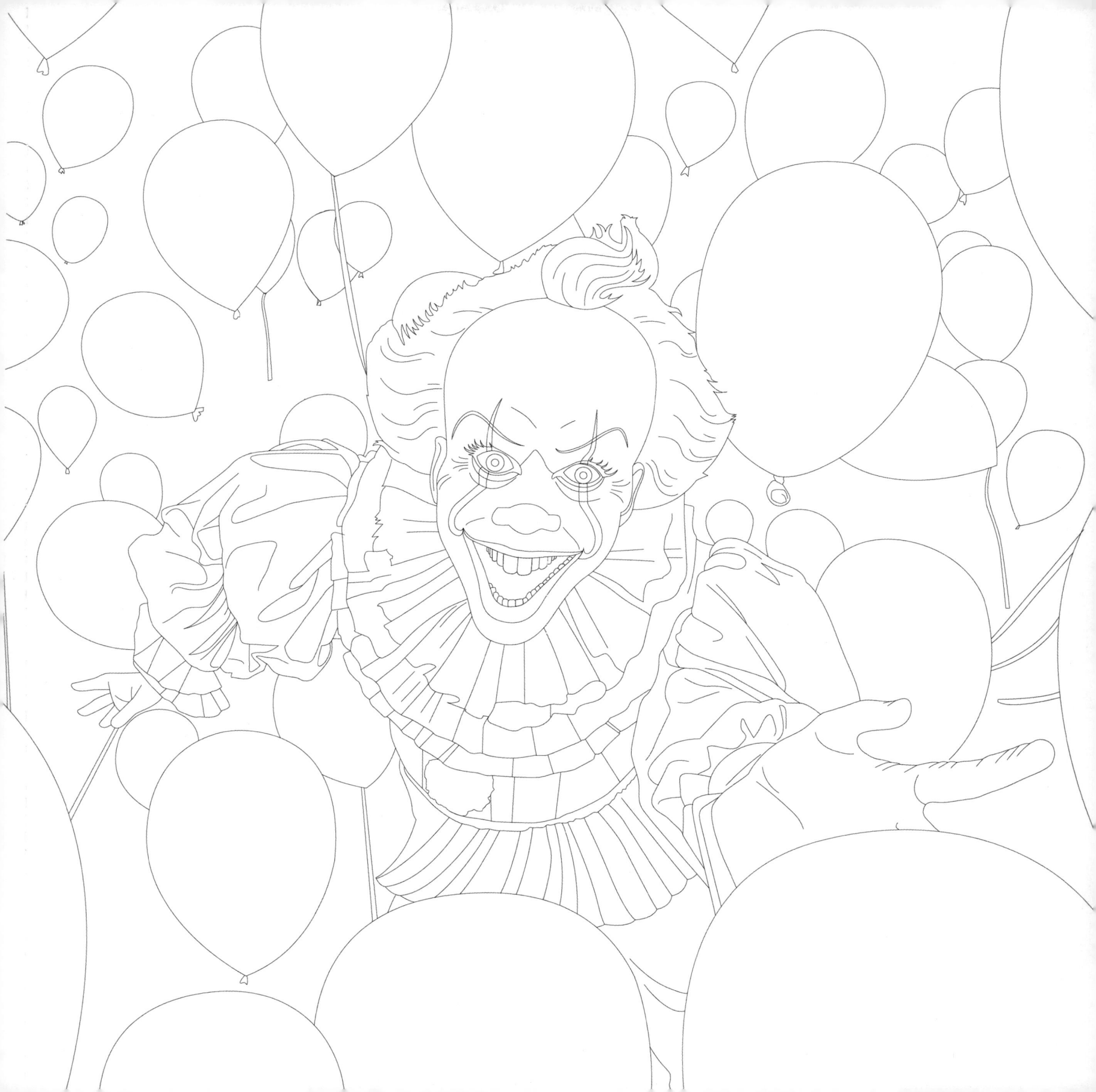

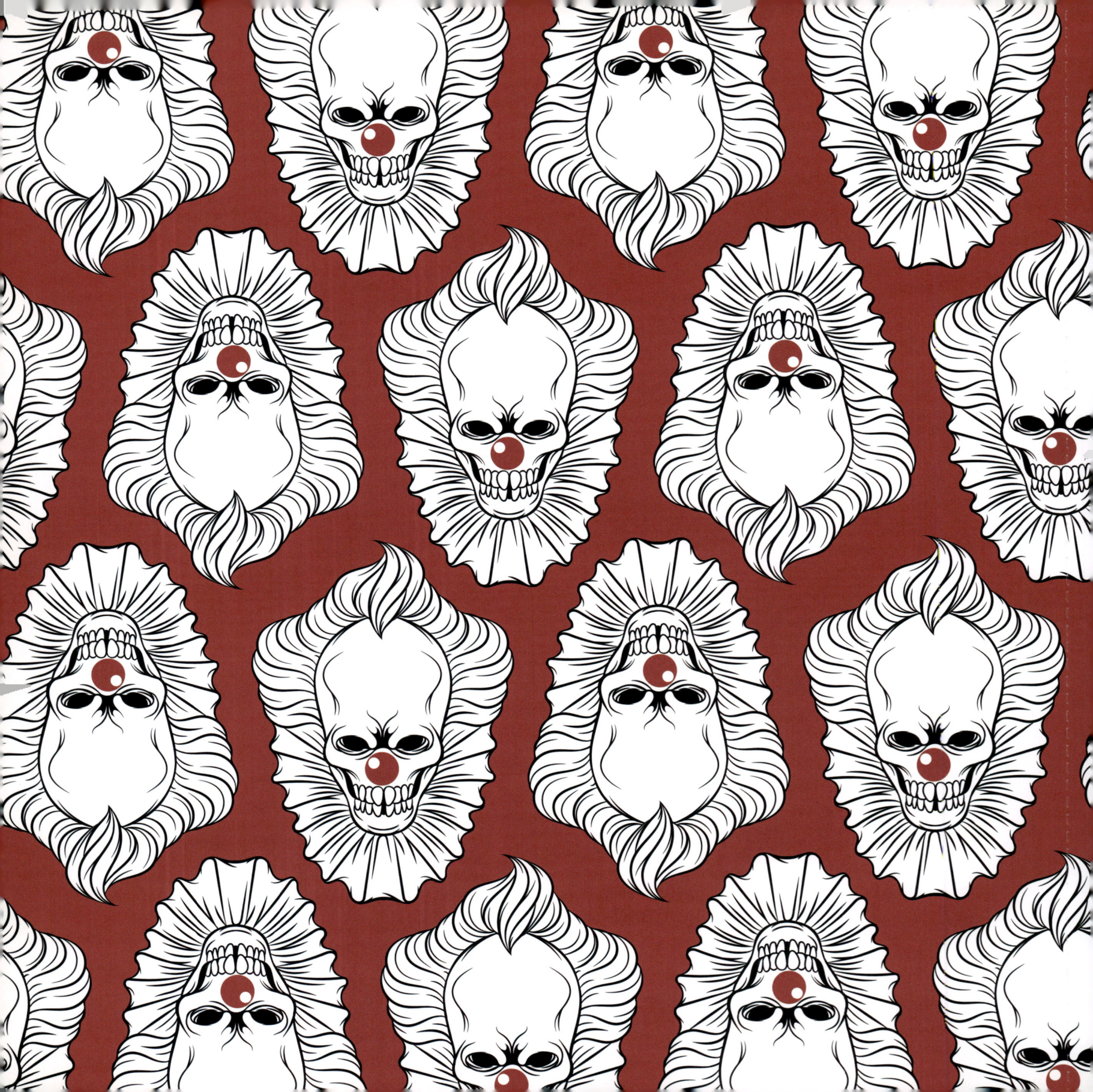

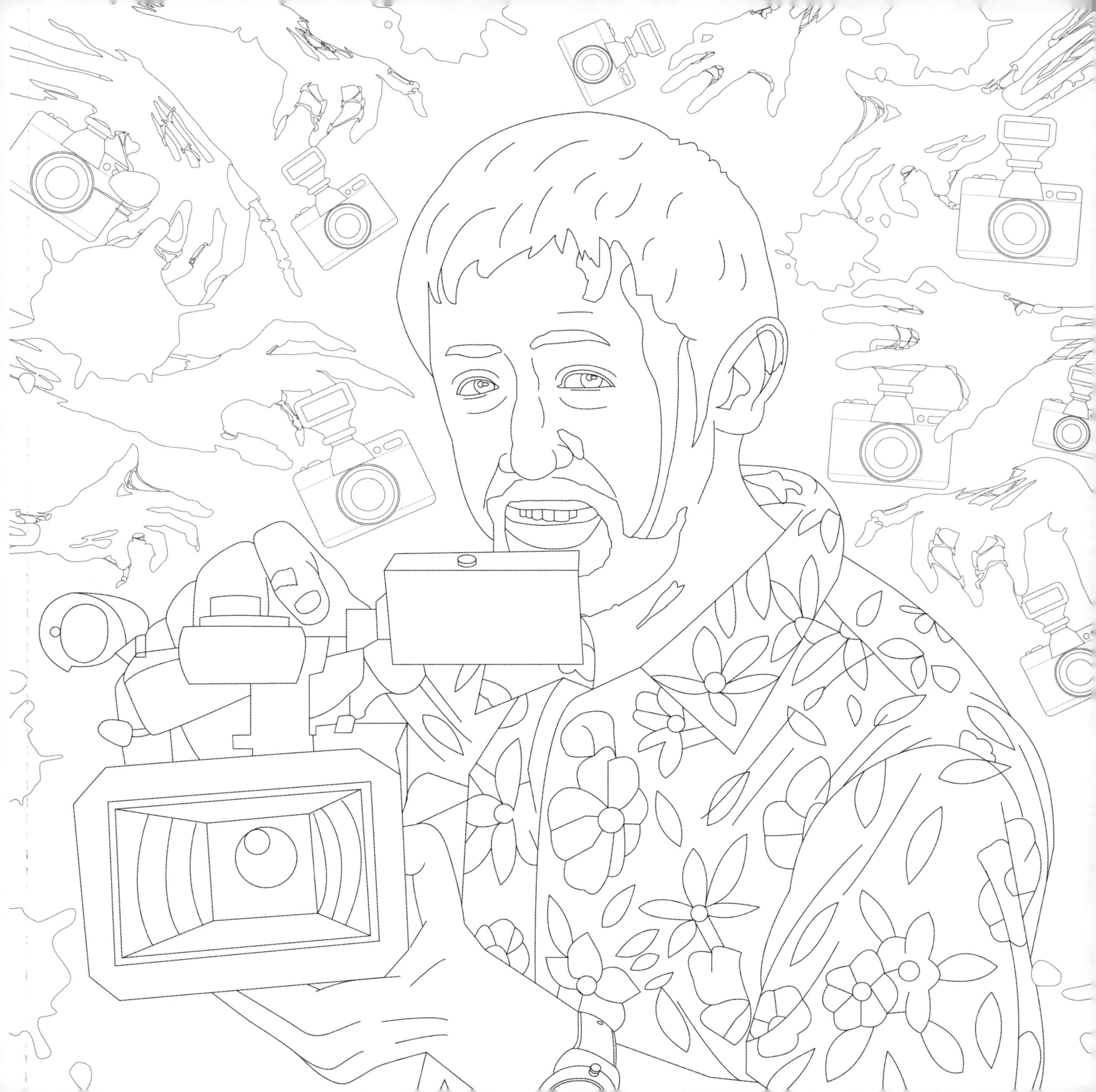

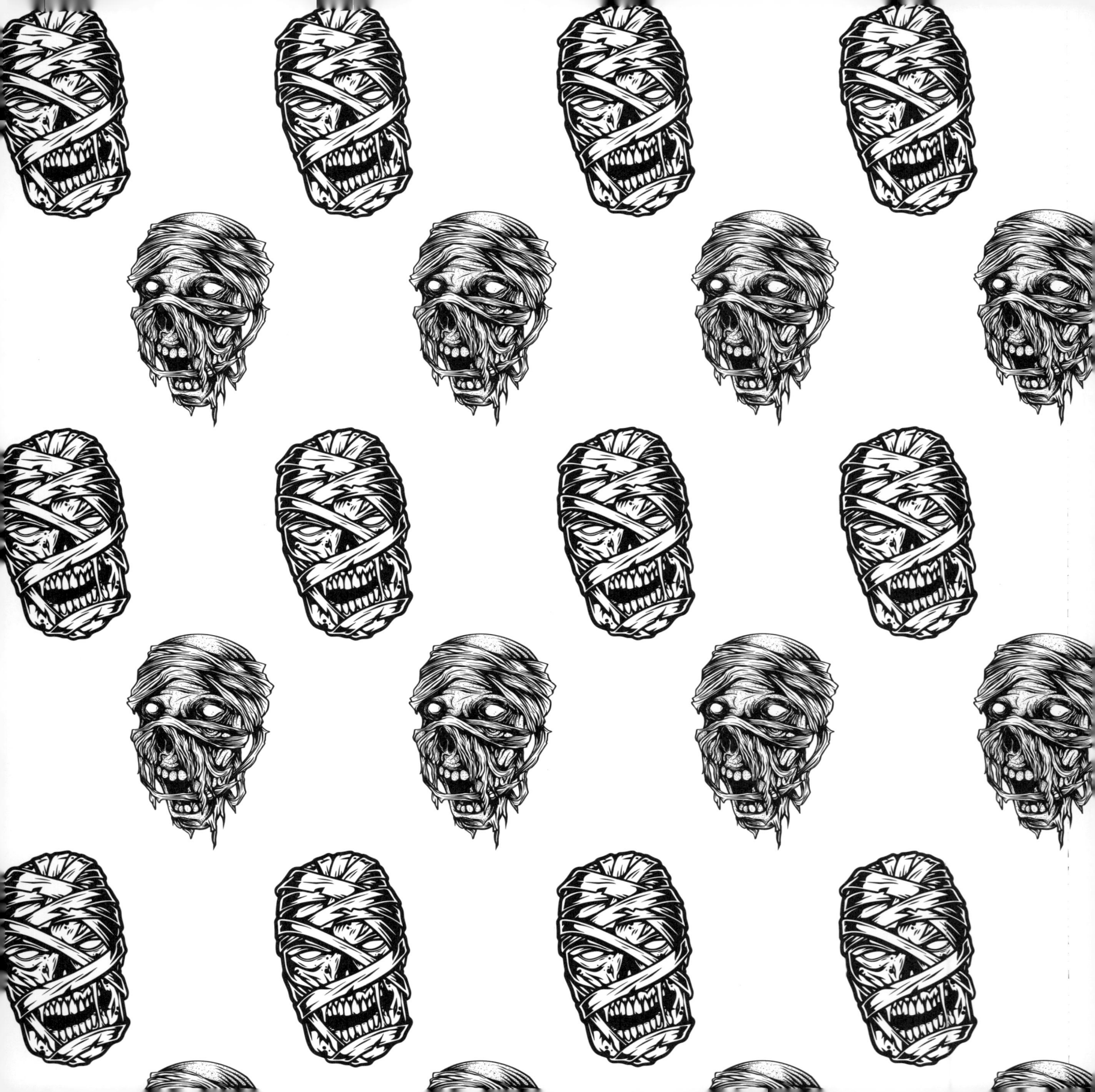

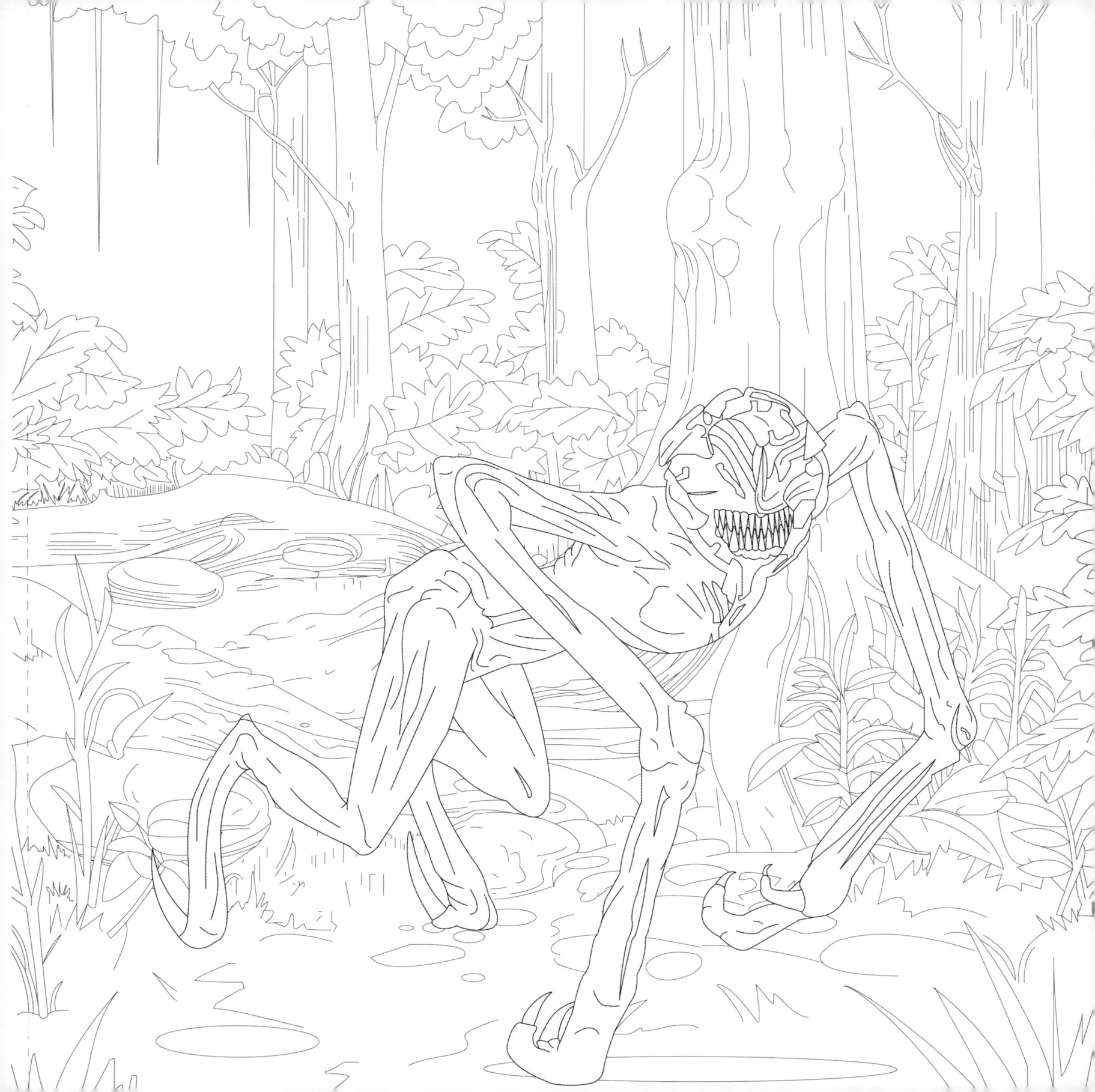

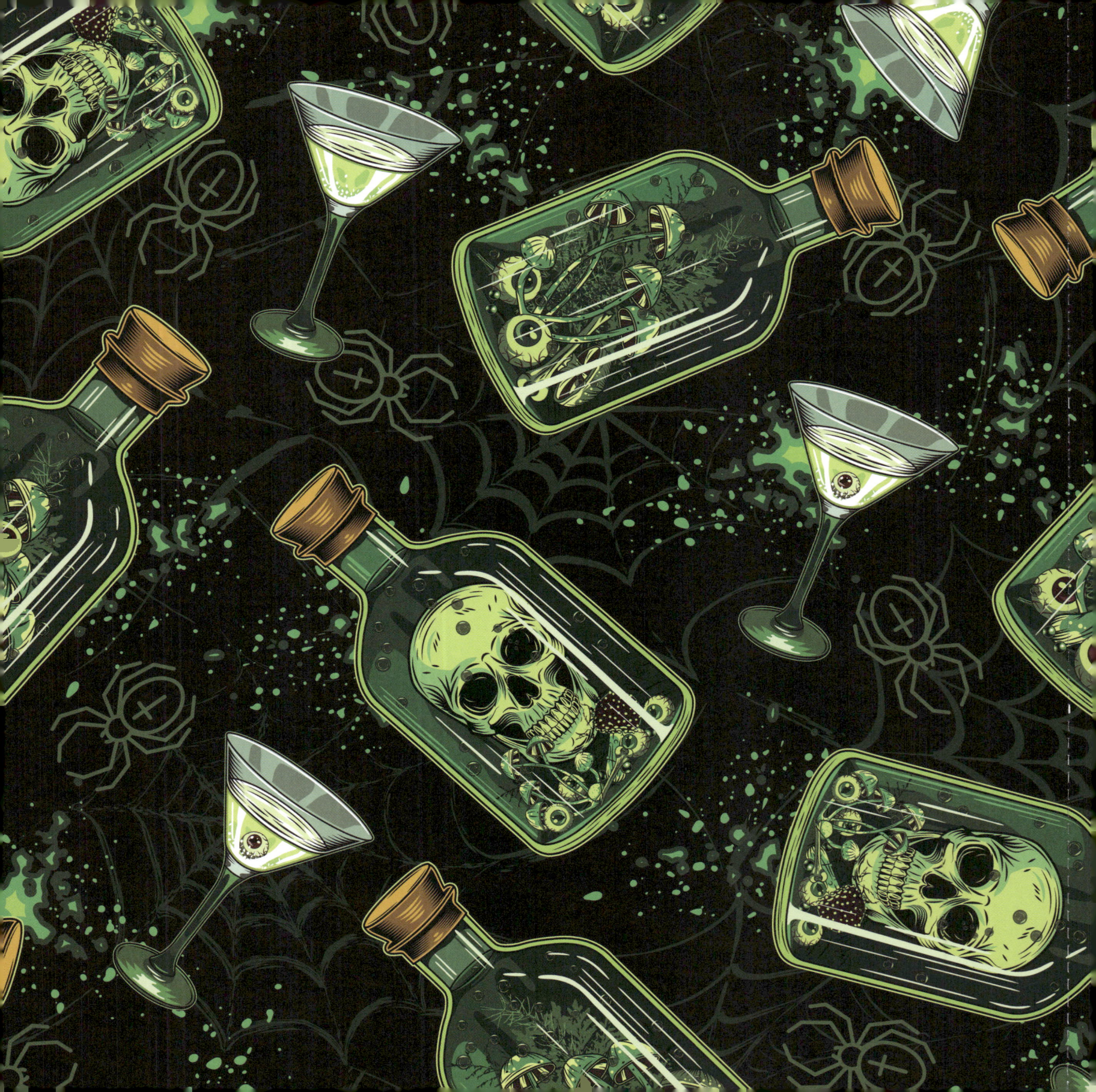

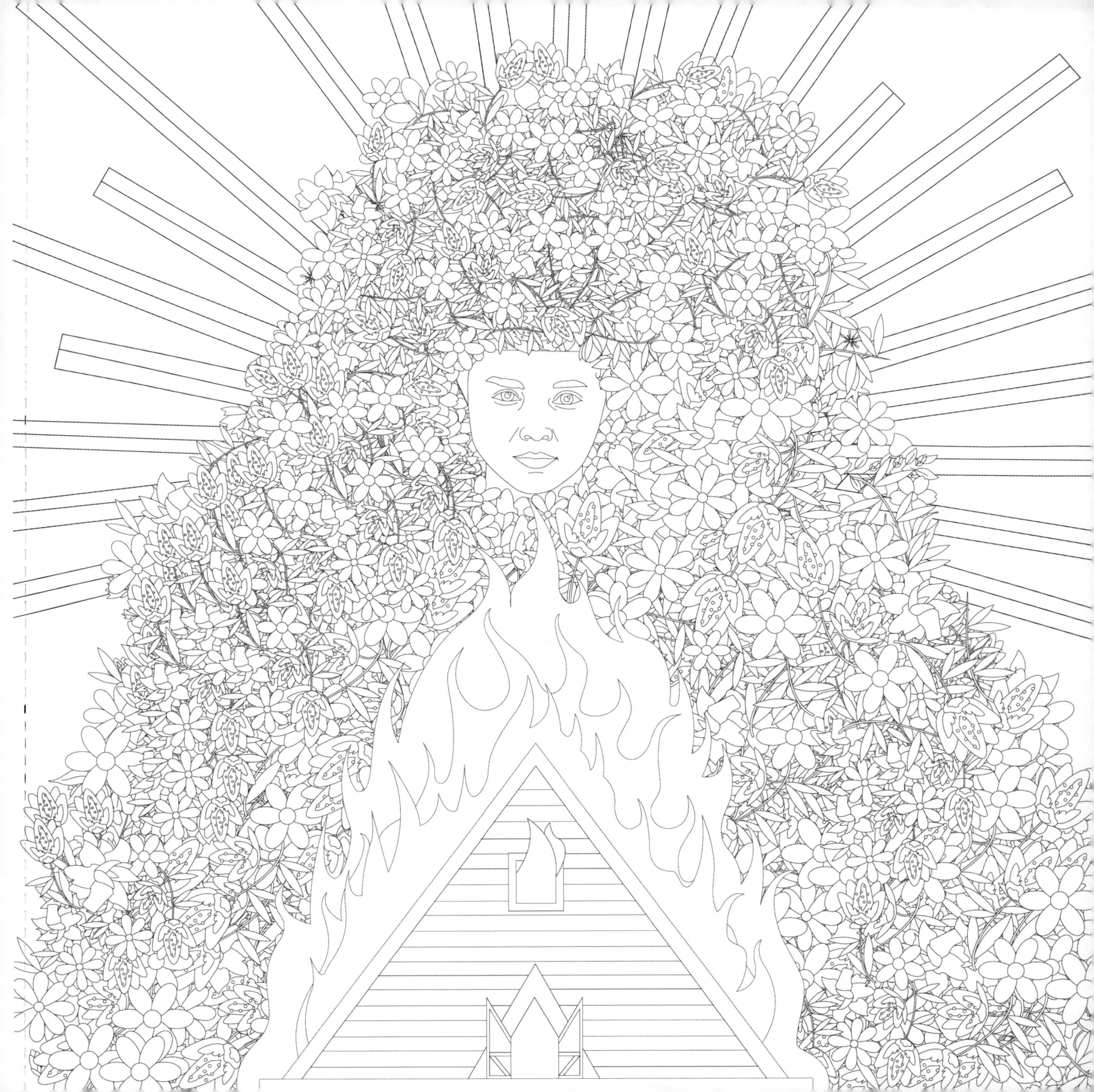

Quarto.com
WalterFoster.com

© 2025 Quarto Publishing Group USA Inc.

First Published in 2025 by Walter Foster Publishing,
an imprint of The Quarto Group,
100 Cummings Center, Suite 265-D, Beverly, MA 01915, USA.
T (978) 282-9590 F (978) 283-2742

All rights reserved. No part of this book may be reproduced in any form without written permission of the copyright owners. All images in this book have been reproduced with the knowledge and prior consent of the artists concerned, and no responsibility is accepted by producer, publisher, or printer for any infringement of copyright or otherwise, arising from the contents of this publication. Every effort has been made to ensure that credits accurately comply with the information supplied. We apologize for any inaccuracies that may have occurred and will resolve inaccurate or missing information in a subsequent reprinting of the book.

Walter Foster Publishing titles are also available at discount for retail, wholesale, promotional, and bulk purchase. For details, contact the Special Sales Manager by email at specialsales@quarto.com or by mail at The Quarto Group, Attn: Special Sales Manager, 100 Cummings Center, Suite 265-D, Beverly, MA 01915, USA.

29 28 27 26 25   1 2 3 4 5

ISBN: 978-0-7603-9710-7

Cover Design: Tanya Jacobson
Illustration: Simon and Sons ITES Services Private Limited
Image Research: Julia DaSilva-Novotny
Page Layout: McKenna Johnson
Patterns sourced from Shutterstock.com

Printed in China

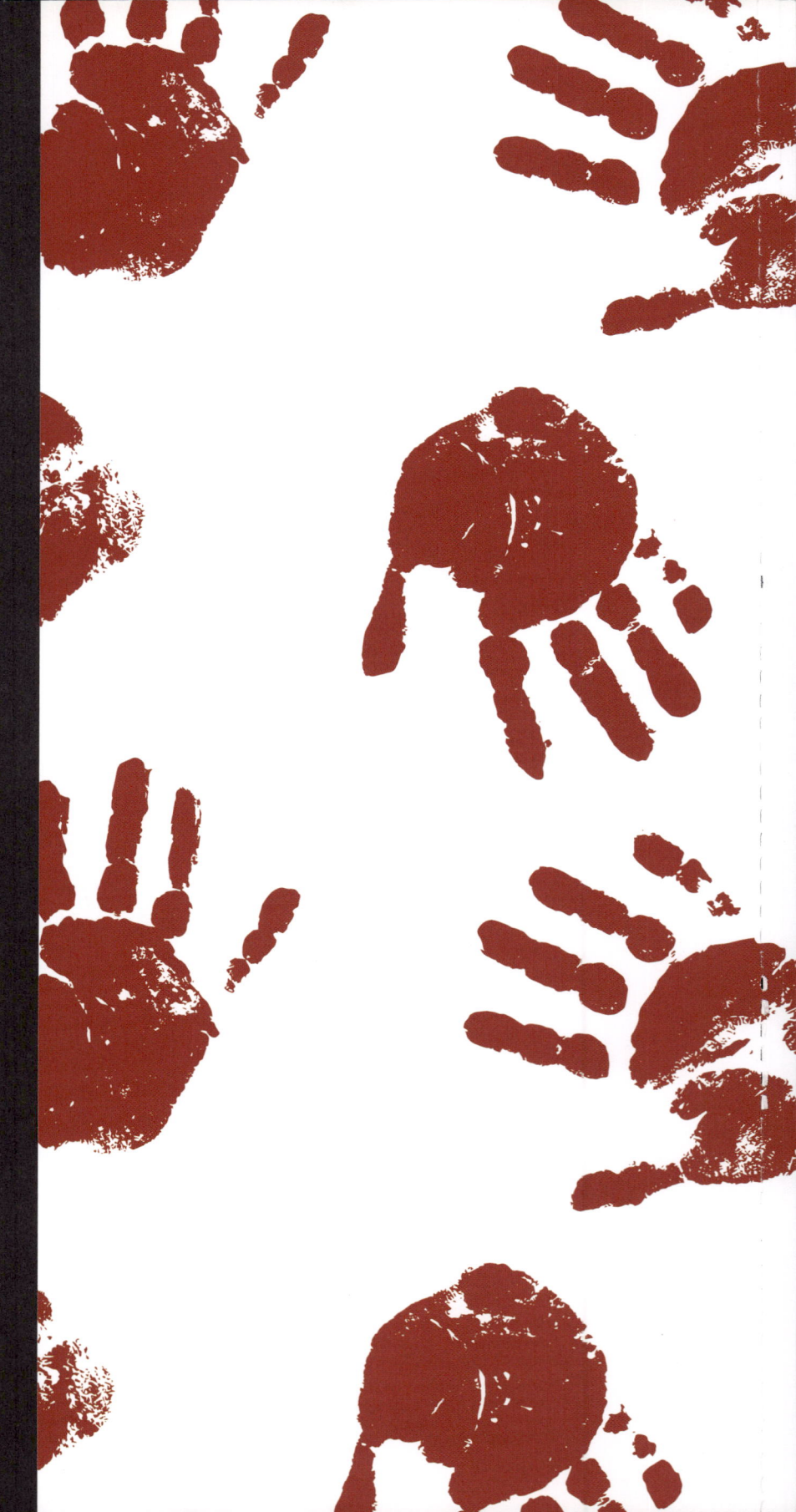